Good Housekeeping

Wine Book

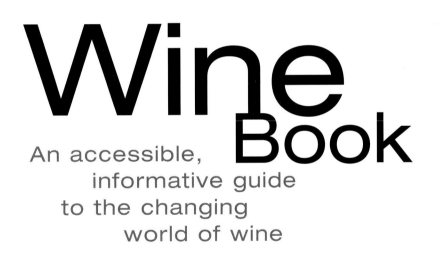

Good Housekeeping

Wine
Book

An accessible,
informative guide
to the changing
world of wine

Jonathan Pedley

Grafton

This edition specially produced for DMG Ltd. in 2002

First published in 2001 by
HarperCollins*Publishers*
77–85 Fulham Palace Road
London W6 8JB

The HarperCollins website address is:
www.**fire**and**water.**com

05 04 03 02 01 00
9 8 7 6 5 4 3 2 1

Published in association with The National Magazine Company Limited
Good Housekeeping is a registered trade mark of
The National Magazine Company Limited

The Good Housekeeping website address is:
www.goodhousekeeping.com

The expression Good Housekeeping as used in the title of the book is
the mark of the National Magazine Company Limited and the Hearst
Corporation, registered in the United Kingdom and the USA, and other
principal countries in the world, and is the absolute property of the National
Magazine Company and the Hearst Corporation. The use of this trade mark
other than with the express permission of the National Magazine Company
Limited or the Hearst Corporation is strictly prohibited.

A CIP catalogue record for this book is available from the British Library

ISBN: 0 00 766248 3

Colour reproduction by Dot Gradations
Printed and bound in Slovenia

This book is typeset in Helvetica and Helvetica Neue

Contents

foreword

Learning about wine is a fascinating pastime but if you're reading this and thinking you already know what you like, then you might also be asking why bother? Well, for starters, it's true that the more you know the better informed your choice is going to be. Sampling and experimenting with different grape varieties and tasting wines made in different countries is key to expanding your knowledge. Plus, once you know more you will be more likely to enjoy the wine you buy; there is also a higher chance that you'll be able to partner wine successfully with dishes both at home and when you eat out.

However, there's no shortcut to understanding wine – it is constantly evolving, with new bottles appearing on the shelves of off-licences and supermarkets every week. But this book will go some way to laying the foundations.

Here you can learn how to taste (as opposed to just drink) wine, to experience its best qualities; how best to store and serve red and white wines; how to choose the best wine to complement your favourite meal and see how it will enhance the flavours. And – a key feature – you can travel your way through the world's grape varieties to see how they're turned into wine.

Emma Marsden

Emma Marsden
Deputy Cookery Editor
Good Housekeeping

Drinking wine

How to taste wine

The first question to answer about wine tasting is why bother? Why not just swig the stuff? Of course there are wines that are best drunk and then forgotten (although you may wish to remember their names to avoid buying them again). In fact, knowing how to taste properly can greatly enhance your enjoyment and appreciation of wine.

You do not need any special paraphernalia to taste wine properly. A tulip-shaped uncoloured glass will be fine, although you can buy the official ISO tasting glass if you wish. Ideally you want to taste wine under natural diffuse light in a room free from any strong smells.

WRITING A TASTING NOTE

There are at least three good reasons for writing a proper tasting note. Firstly, your description of a wine is a personal *aide-mémoire*. Unless a wine is genuinely unforgettable, its characteristics, and even its name and vintage, will soon be forgotten. What is more, a good tasting note will allow you to describe a wine to somebody else. Secondly, noting down all the characteristics of the wines you drink may well allow you to discern a pattern about the wines you like or dislike. For instance, if you discover that you do not get along with white wines that have high acidity, or that are very oaky, you can alter your buying decisions accordingly. This approach will make you more conscious of the subtleties that distinguish one wine from another. Finally, with some practice you can start to make an objective appraisal of the quality of the wine. This may not alter your buying decisions in the short term, but all our tastes continually evolve and you may find that a wine that

was not to your taste a few years ago becomes a favourite as time passes.

When tasting wine you deploy three of your senses: sight, smell and taste. Hence a tasting sheet usually has headings of Appearance, Nose and Palate. There is usually a space for Conclusions at the end as well.

Appearance

It is always worth trying to judge the appearance of a wine against a white background. The first thing to check is whether the wine is clear and bright. Any cloudiness or dullness about the appearance may indicate that the wine is faulted (*see page 26*). The next thing to note is the depth of colour of the wine. Some wines are naturally relatively pale in colour, for example Frascati is often almost water white, whilst amongst the black grapes Pinot Noir makes lightish red wines. By contrast, Sauternes is usually deep in colour for a white wine, and reds made from grapes like Cabernet Sauvignon and Shiraz can be so dark that they are virtually opaque.

Having made some comment about the intensity of the colour, have a stab at describing the wine's actual hue. The main descriptions used for white wines are: straw, lemon and gold, whilst for reds they are: purple, pink, ruby, garnet, brick and tawny. With red wines, as well as commenting on the colour in the centre of the glass where the wine is at its deepest, you should tip the glass up and have a look at the hue on the rim. The colour on the rim gives you a feel for the age of a red wine. Young red wines will be purple or pink on the rim. With ageing wine you will start to see more orange and brown on the rim, the colour eventually fading towards brick and tawny. If you are tasting a sparkling wine then a note should also be made of the amount of fizz (*mousse*) and the size of the bubbles (the tinier the better).

Nose

If you just hold the glass up to your nose and snort you should pick up some aromas straight-away. However, by swirling the wine around the glass and then snorting you will get a much bigger hit of smell. Hard core wine tasters tend to swirl their wine as a matter of instinct – useful for dis-guising the fact that they couldn't hold a glass still if they tried. The first thing to check on the nose is: does the wine smell clean and fresh? Dirty, mouldy or varnishy smells tell you that the wine is faulted (*see page 26*). Assuming everything is in order, make a note of the intensity of the smell. It requires a bit of practice to establish the grada-tions of aroma intensity. However, white wines like Soave tend to have a very delicate nose, while at the other extreme Alsace Gewurztraminer can sometimes blow the back of your head off.

Having commented on the intensity of the nose, you need to have a stab at actually describ-ing the wine's smell. For many people this is the most intimidating part of wine tasting. One way to get started is to think of a wine's aroma breaking down into three main types of smell:

Fruit After all, the stuff should have been made out of grapes.

Floral Some wines are distinctly perfumed and scented.

Earthy / spicy Often associated with old wines, or wines that have been aged in oak.

Once you have identified one or more of these families of smell, the brave might want to try and push things one stage further. If you thought the wine was fruity, floral or spicy, ask yourself what sort of fruit, flowers or spices spring to mind as you smell the wine. It is one of the magical things about wine that you can get hints of all sorts of aromas on the nose, as well as the obvious smells that derive from the grapes. Some clever

Assessing the appearance, nose and palate of a wine. Drawing air into the mouth (bottom left) when tasting a wine can help release the aromas.

The evolution of colour in red wine. On the left is a young red, on the right is an old red.

research has found that some of the descriptions are not as fanciful as they seem. The leafy, gooseberry aroma associated with the Sauvignon Blanc grape seems to be caused by a group of aromatic compounds called methoxypyrazines, which are naturally present in this particular variety. Whether they also remind the taster of running naked through a nettle patch to escape from a pile of burning tyres is a matter of conjecture.

Palate

Having spent so much time on the appearance and the nose you will be gagging for a taste of the wine. The first thing to note on the palate is the level of sweetness. If there is no sugar present then the wine is dry (e.g. Chablis). 'Medium' is the description applied to wines that have some sweetness (e.g. Liebfraumilch), whereas 'sweet'

indicates a wine containing a large amount of sugar (e.g. Sauternes).

The next thing to comment on is the acidity. You taste acid on the sides of your tongue. Some wines like Muscadet tend to be high in acidity, whereas your average Australian Chardonnay is relatively low in acidity.

The third element of the palate is the alcohol. You can gauge the alcohol level of a wine not so much through taste as through the warming sensation the alcohol creates in the mouth and throat. Around 12.5% alcohol by volume (ABV) is the global average for wine, and at this strength a taster will be conscious of a gentle warmness in the mouth. Once you get to 13.5%ABV or more the wine will have a distinctly 'hot', peppery burn. By contrast, as the alcohol level drops below 11%ABV you become barely conscious of the alcohol, the flavour becoming more like fruit juice.

Describing the body of a wine is an almost instinctive thing. Some wines, like Valpolicella, have a light-bodied texture in the mouth, whilst others, such as serious Australian Shiraz, are rich and full-bodied.

Staying with reds, the longer you keep the wine in your mouth the more you will be conscious of a sandy, gum-drying sensation. What you are experiencing are the tannins in the wine coating your gums, tongue and teeth. Tannins are naturally occurring compounds, extracted from black grape skins at the same time as the red colour. The tannin level of red wines varies markedly. For instance, the Gamay grape tends to have fairly soft tannins, whereas Cabernet Sauvignon grapes are very tannic.

Just as you commented on any obvious aromas on the nose, so you may wish to note any distinctive flavours that come through on the palate. Once you have swallowed (or spat out) the wine, ponder how long the flavour of the wine persists in your mouth. The flavour of simple wines is often gone very quickly, whereas the finish on really great wines goes on and on.

Conclusions

The first part of the conclusion of a tasting note involves trying to get an objective fix on the quality of a wine. There is always a danger, not confined to wine, of associating quality with personal preference. I may find Renoir's paintings insipid and tedious but that does not mean he was a 'bad' artist. Similarly, you personally may not like sweet wines, but that does not mean a particular Sauternes is a poor wine. There are two main pointers to the quality of a wine: the complexity of the nose and the length of the finish. The more complex the nose (in other words, the more different types of smell you can pick up), and the longer the flavour stays in your mouth, the better the wine. You may wish to factor price in as well. It is unrealistic to expect cheap wines to have any great complexity or length. Equally, if an expensive bottle does not deliver real complexity and a long finish then it represents poor value for money. Magazines will often score wines out of 20 or 100 to allow consumers to see the relative quality of the bottles under review.

The second part of the conclusion involves thinking about the wine's maturity. This is not so much to do with the age of a wine as with its drinkability. Wines go through three stages of maturity: too young (when they can be thought of as being a bit raw and angular), drinking well (when the wine's components are in harmony), or 'drying out' (when the wine's fruit has faded leaving a dried-out skeleton). Of course most of the wines that the average consumer will encounter are likely to be drinking well at the time of sale. It

Tasting notes

Name of wine	Riesling, Cuvée Frédéric Emile, Trimbach 1996
Appearance	Clear and bright. Mid-intensity of colour. Straw.
Nose	Clean and fresh. Fairly intense aroma. Green fruit: apple and quince. Great finesse, but with a stony, austere edge.
Palate	Dry, high acidity, mid-high alcohol. Light-bodied and tightly structured. Lemon and cooking apple. A real zip on the mid-palate. Long finish.
Conclusion	**Quality:** the complexity of the nose and the length of the finish indicate very good quality. **Maturity:** drinking well now, but has the fruit and acidity to keep for at least another five years. **Food:** magic with trout and other river fish.

requires a bit of practice to take the analysis of maturity a stage further and start to predict the future life of a wine. If a white wine is going to age well it usually needs plenty of fruit backed up by a high acidity content. This is the reason why many of the great German Rieslings can age so gracefully, whilst most of the Spanish white wines are best enjoyed as young as possible. Red wines, by contrast, are generally held together by fruit and tannin. Great Bordeaux wines have these elements in abundance and so age very well. Beaujolais has the fruit, but the lack of tannin limits its capacity to age.

You may wish to finish the conclusion by thinking about what sort of food might work well with the wine being tasted (*see page 22*).

How to buy wine

There are certainly plenty of different options when it comes to purchasing wine nowadays. From the latest cyber wine shop to the horny-handed peasant who wrung the stuff from the earth (and appreciates the cash, no questions asked), we are spoilt for choice as consumers.

OFF TRADE AND ON TRADE

Those operations where you buy your wine to take away with you (e.g. supermarkets and off-licences) are referred to as the off trade. The on trade is composed of outlets where you buy and drink your booze on the retail premises (e.g. restaurants and pubs).

Supermarkets

In the UK, the off trade has come to dominate wine sales. What is more, within the off trade the big supermarket groups have a huge chunk of the market. It is after all the supermarkets that have done more than anyone else to make wine an everyday part of the grocery basket. Most of the larger stores carry an impressive range of wines from around the world. The supermarkets' great strength tends to be in the inexpensive and mid-priced part of the wine price spectrum (in the UK, between £2.50 and about £8). As well as their own-label products, there is a lot of focus on the major branded producers (particularly in the New World ranges).

Off-licences

In recent years, the off-licence sector has been something of a poor relation compared with the power of the supermarkets. In fact, the range and quality of wine stocked by off-licences varies from limited and dire to comprehensive and stunning. It is worth doing some reconnaissance work in your neighbourhood to discover whether you have a decent off-licence. As well as its wines, a good off-licence should have a knowledgeable and enthusiastic manager and staff. Quality people in a shop can make all the difference. They can offer advice, tutor tastings, introduce you to new lines and help with food and wine combinations. Off-licences struggle to match the supermarkets at the cheap end of the price spectrum. However, in the mid-priced bracket (£5 to £8) they are often strong, and the better ones will have a good selection of premium wines (over £8), including some esoteric lines that the supermarkets cannot justify carrying.

Wine merchants

Most of the sophisticated wine merchants do much of their business through mail-order. The top players have wine lists that are packed full with background information about the wines that are stocked. The ranges are often enormous, starting at mid-market prices and going up as far as your credit limit will go. These are the people to approach if you want to stock up on some of the world's top estate wines, which are inevitably available only in small quantities and for high prices. If you give them a telephone call you can usually get hold of someone who not only knows what the wine you are interested in tastes like, but they are probably the godfather of the grower's youngest son and can give you chapter and verse on how the wine was made.

The Internet

The Internet has opened up another channel for wine retailing. Whilst there are a number of pure Internet wine merchants, existing supermarkets, off-licences and mail-order companies have in many cases added an online facility. There is no reason why the range carried by an Internet merchant cannot be updated with new wines and offers on a daily basis. What is more, once the capital required to set up the operation has been spent, the running costs should be relatively modest. As with a traditional mail-order wine merchant, deliveries are to your door. To avoid excessive delivery charges it is best to order by the 12-bottle case (which can usually be mixed).

Auction houses and brokers

If you become a fine wine buff then you will end up buying (and also selling) some of your wines through the auction houses or wine brokers. The principal auction houses have a programme of wine sales in London, New York and other major cities in the USA, Europe and Asia. Rather than offering set piece auctions every few weeks, the fine wine brokers buy and sell wine on a daily basis. Auction houses and brokers are one of the main routes for buying fine Clarets, Ports and other old, rare or fashionable wines.

Buying direct from the winery

What an increasing number of people are doing is visiting the grower or winery and buying literally at the cellar door. You get to see where the wine was made, sometimes meet the person who crafted it, and perhaps most important of all, you

www.decanter.com is not a retailer itself, but many of the wines recommended on the site (and in *Decanter* magazine) can be purchased online.

can usually taste a selection of wines before making your choice. Idyllic as this all sounds, it is worth mentioning a couple of caveats. Whilst you are under no legal obligation to buy after having spent an hour with a grower tasting his life's work, cowards like me will feel the moral obligation of buying a few bottles even if the liquid they contain is not worthy of being poured over fish and chips. The other important point is that if you are on holiday undergoing some sort of bucolic trip worthy of Virgil's *Georgics*, pinch yourself before buying a grower's total production. What can taste fantastic on its home patch when you are in a relaxed mood may not show so well six months later on a cold and rainy Tuesday night with chicken and mushroom pie.

A very useful aid to buying direct is to get hold of one of the annual guides covering the wine region you are visiting. For example, *Le Guide Hachette des Vins* lists thousands of recommended growers in France (see *Recommended Reading on page 186* for similar books covering other countries). As well as the address and telephone number of each property, details of opening hours are shown and there is a guide to the sort of prices you can expect to pay.

Fact Box

Mandatory information
The wine's country of origin.
The bottler's name and address.
Percentage alcohol by volume.
The size of the bottle.
A lot number.
The quality status of the wine (which may include its region of origin).

Optional information
Varietal composition.
Vintage date.
The wine's style (e.g. sweet, rosé).
Brand name.
Awards and medals.
Serving suggestions (e.g. 'serve chilled').

Hotels and restaurants

Although the off trade dwarfs the on trade in terms of UK wine sales, the on trade has seen decent growth in recent years. In tandem with increasing volume of sales, the on trade has had to adapt itself to the modern wine market. There was a time when top hotels and restaurants had wine lists dominated by the classic regions of Europe: Bordeaux, Mosel, Port etc. Much of this wine was bought when it was young and then laid down in the establishment's cellar until it was mature. Nowadays, very few hotels can afford to tie up so much capital in stock. What is more, the vibrant New World wines are capturing an ever-growing share of wine lists.

Pubs and clubs

The pub and club trade has experienced an even bigger revolution when it comes to wine. Not so long ago many pubs rather reluctantly carried a limited range of wines. The wines were often not that thrilling to start with, and their storage and service sometimes left a lot to be desired. This, however, has changed for the better. Today's pub operators are interested in being successful retailers, rather than just being outlets for dispensing a brewery's production. As long as there is money

to be made from it, modern pubs are as happy selling cappuccinos, mozzarella salads and wines such as Chilean Chardonnay as they are pulling pints of draught beer.

READING THE LABEL

Having found an outlet that sells interesting wines, the next challenge is to try to understand the labels. It is still possible to come across labels that seem to have been designed to create confusion in the mind and strike terror in the heart of a potential purchaser.

Design aside, the European Union's (EU) rules on wine labelling are relatively straightforward. The mandatory items are: the wine's country of origin; the bottler's name and address; percentage alcohol by volume; the size of the bottle; a lot number and the quality status of the wine (which may include its region of origin).

If the wine was produced outside the EU and then shipped in, the labels must also show the importer's name and address. For wines that are made in the EU, the quality status will be either

Two different approaches to the labelling of German wines. I know I should prefer the clean minimalism of the label on the right, but I prefer the label on the left.

'Table Wine' or 'Quality Wine Produced in a Specified Region' (this is obviously expressed in accor-
dance with the local regime and in the local
language; *see pages 68, 113, 119, 127, 136*).
Wines that are brought in from outside the EU are
either described as just 'Wine', or they may show
a geographical description such as 'Barossa' or
'Napa Valley'.

Optional items of information that may appear
on a label include: the varietal composition; the
vintage date; the wine's style (e.g. sweet or rosé);
the brand name; any awards and medals; and
some serving suggestions (e.g. 'serve chilled').

Many wines also indicate if they were bottled
at the estate where they were produced. A lot of
the world's finest wines are bottled in this way, so
it is worth looking out for 'Mis en bouteille au
château / domaine / à la propriété', 'Gutsabfüllung'
or 'Estate Bottled'.

These strict rules about what can and cannot
appear on a wine label apply only to the front
label. By contrast, producers have a fairly free
hand about the text that can appear on the back
label. Hence many commercially astute producers
use the back label to give some information about
the wine's production (e.g. aged in oak barrels for
nine months), what it tastes like, as well as some
suggested food combinations.

BOTTLE SHAPES

There was a time when it was possible to generalise about bottle shapes. With the rise of the
'designer' bottle, it is now virtually impossible to
identify a wine solely based on its bottle shape.
However, a significant amount of wine is still
bottled in three particular shapes of bottle: the
high-shouldered 'Bordeaux' bottle; the sloping-
shouldered 'Burgundy' bottle and the tall, thin
'Germanic' flute bottle.

Classic bottle shapes. From left
to right: 'Burgundy', 'Germanic'
flute and 'Bordeaux'.

How to store and serve wine

There are a number of 'rules' and conventions about the storage and service of wine. At their heart is the fragility of wine. Stored incorrectly or served in a blasé fashion, even the greatest wine in the world can be ruined.

STORING WINE

For those of us who do not have access to a cellar with perfect conditions, do not despair. If you are going to drink a wine within six months of purchase you can usually get away with stashing it in a utility room, outside toilet, under the stairs or at the bottom of a cupboard. You can buy temperature- and humidity-controlled wine storage cabinets for bottles that you want to keep for an extended period. If you start to buy serious quantities of wine, you will find that many fine wine merchants can arrange storage (for an annual fee).

Cellaring wine

There is still something of a myth, that by laying down any bottle of wine it will automatically improve in the cellar. This was never true, and certainly is not the case nowadays. Most wines today are made in a direct, fruit-driven style for consumption within a year or two of the harvest. Long cellaring will only lead them to become flat, flabby and ultimately oxidised.

If you want to build up a cellar then it makes sense to focus on the wines that are built to last. Amongst the red wines, go for things like Vintage Port, top Clarets and concentrated New World Cabernet Sauvignons. Age-worthy white wines include fine German Rieslings and Sauternes. It is always worth trying to buy several bottles of anything you are going to lay down. This will allow you to pull out and enjoy bottles of the wine as it matures, at the same time getting a fix on whether the other bottles should be drunk up soon or be kept for longer.

Cellaring a wine for several years can achieve two things. Great young wines can have intense fruit and oak aromas, but the nose is often a bit raw, jammy and disjointed. With bottle age the immediate fruitiness and oakiness will evolve into a complex bouquet with more mellow traits. Similarly, the palate of a young red wine can often be rather tough and foursquare. A few years in the cellar will smooth off the tannins and should result in a more harmonious wine.

SERVING WINE

Serving wine at the right temperature is a worry for many people. Some guidelines are shown below, but it is worth being aware how temperature affects the aroma and flavour of wine. As far as the nose of a wine is concerned, the higher the service temperature, the more aromas will be released. If you serve a wine over-chilled you will lose most of the smell (this is why really vile white wine should be served as cold as possible). However, higher temperatures will also result in more alcohol evaporating. This can cause a wine to smell raw and spirity. On the palate, low temperatures seem to exaggerate the acidity and tannin content of wine, but play down its alcohol and

Fact Box

Storing wine

Maintain a cool, even temperature.

Avoid strong light.

Avoid movement.

Avoid strong smells.

Avoid humidity.

Lay bottles on their sides.

Guidelines for storage

Maintain the bottles at a cool, even temperature

Around 12°C (54°F) is about right. If the temperature is a tad higher than this all is not lost, but be aware that the wine's evolution will be more rapid. What should be avoided are any violent swings of temperature. I have seen the corks forced out of bottles that were brought from the cellar and placed on a table outdoors in the summer. The rapid rise in temperature causes the volume of the wine to increase, pushing the corks out.

Avoid any strong light

Light energy can speed up a lot of the chemical reactions that can cause wine to deteriorate.

Avoid any movement or vibration

Movement will dislodge the sediment in old red wines. There is also the worry with very old bottles that movement may put pressure on an already decrepit cork.

Avoid any strong smells

There is a theoretical risk that strong smells may taint wine. However, if the cork is forming an airtight seal there should be no problem.

Avoid humidity

A very humid environment will encourage the labels to rot, and some capsules will corrode.

Lay the bottles on their sides

This will ensure that the corks are kept moist and maintain a good seal. In these conditions a good-quality natural cork can protect the wine for 30+ years. For wines that are going to receive very long cellaring it is possible to have the bottles re-corked after several decades. Laying bottles on their sides is better than storing them upside down. The problem with storing bottles cork-down is that if any sediment or tartrate crystals *(see page 27)* form, a blockage can occur up against the cork. With screw-top bottles there is no point in storing them on their sides, so they can stand proudly next to your bottles of gin. There was a debate a few years ago about whether Champagne needed to be laid on its side for storage. There was much talk of saturated gases etc., but given that there seems to be no disadvantage in laying the bottles down, why take the risk?

Fact Box

Wine serving temperatures

17°C (67°F)
mid-and full-bodied red wines.

12°C (54°F)
light-bodied red wines, fine dry white wines.

8°C (46°F)
simpler dry white wines, sweet white wines, rosé wines.

4°C (40°F)
sparkling wines.

sugar content. Warmer temperatures have the opposite effect. This is one of the main reasons for serving tannic red wines at room temperature.

Glasses

The subject of what type of wine glasses to use is the cause of much debate. There are companies that have devised glasses tailor-made to specific wine styles (although I have not seen a Liebfraumilch glass yet). A decent sized, plain, uncoloured, tulip-shaped glass will be fine for most wines. In fact, as an omni-usage wine glass, the ISO tasting glass is not a bad option. You may also wish to have some flute glasses for sparkling wines (throw out those sad saucer-shaped ones from the 1960s). Beware of becoming too

anoraky about glasses – at some level they are just a conveyance for getting the alcohol from the bottle to the mouth.

Corkscrews

Corkscrews are another area that seems to have been the focus of a disproportionate amount of human time and ingenuity. Some of the more complicated ones look as if they were devised for use in the Lubyanka rather than a restaurant. Several designs work well, it is just a matter of experimenting and finding the one you are happiest with. Always cut off the top of the capsule before inserting the corkscrew. This allows you to wipe away any gunge or mould, and gives the bottle a neat appearance when served.

Decanting

One other element of wine service where people differ in approach is over when to decant a wine, and the related process of letting a wine breathe (opening the bottle an hour or so before drinking it). These operations bear on two separate issues concerning wine service: the removal of sediment and the effect of aeration on the aroma and flavour of a wine.

Where a red wine has a heavy sediment, it will normally make sense to decant. Vintage Port is the most obvious example. If you are going to decant a wine, stand the bottle upright the day before to allow any loose sediment to settle. Once you have opened the bottle, pour the wine carefully into the receiving decanter (or another clean bottle). If the wine you are decanting is in a dark bottle, you can check if the sediment is moving by placing a lit candle under the neck of the bottle to illuminate the wine. Once sediment starts to shift, stop decanting. Any dregs can be recovered by filtering through a coffee filter or a pair of tights.

Temperature guidelines

Most mid- and full-bodied red wines should be served at room temperature, around 17°C (67°F). It is worth remembering that the idea of serving wine at room temperature was developed in the days before central heating. Many houses nowadays are maintained at tropical temperature levels, far too warm for everything except mulled wine.

Light-bodied reds with relatively low tannin levels (such as Beaujolais and Valpolicella) can be served at cellar temperature, 12°C (54°F).

Fine dry white wines should be served at cellar temperature, 12°C (54°F). The number of posh restaurants that insist on serving £70 bottles of white Burgundy from the ice bucket is surprisingly high. **Simpler dry white wines** can be chilled slightly to around 8°C (46°F). **Sweet white wines and rosés** should also be served at this temperature.

Sparkling wines should be chilled right down to 4°C (40°F). There is a safety issue with sparkling wines in that the lower the temperature of the wine, the lower the pressure will be in the bottle. Hence there is less chance of the cork flying out if the bottle is well chilled. The old hands in the restaurant trade also recommend keeping a napkin over the cork, and holding the cork firmly whilst turning the bottle.

There is a school of thought that says that letting a red wine breathe opens up its aroma and softens its palate. Some people swear by the efficacy of this technique, others are more sceptical. Certainly the amount of aeration a wine will receive over a couple of hours with an exposed surface area of 2.5 cm² (½ sq in) is limited. The aeration the wine receives as it is poured into the glass and swirled by the drinker may be more than is achieved by letting the wine breathe.

If you really want to aerate your wine, you might as well go the whole hog and decant the bottle, whether it has a sediment or not. It is worth, however, flagging up a note of caution about very old and fragile red wines. Such wines can deteriorate extremely rapidly when exposed to the air, so these should not be decanted even if they have sediment. Pour them very carefully directly into the wine glass, using a wicker bottle holder, if you wish.

The open bottle

In the Pedley household few bottles once opened survive for more than half an hour. However, should you be unable to finish a bottle of wine at one go, the question arises as to how long wine in an open bottle will keep. Most white wines if they are re-corked and then kept in the refrigerator overnight will be in decent shape the following day. Champagne, even without a silver spoon hung in the neck of the bottle or a specialist sparkling wine closure, will retain a decent amount of fizz at breakfast the morning after (this is a seriously useful tip for all the wild livers out there). A young, robust red wine re-corked and then kept in a cool place will usually hold together for a couple of days.

It is of course oxidation that limits the life of a wine once the bottle has been opened (see page 26). Hence there are various pieces of equipment for either creating a vacuum in half-empty wine bottles, or alternatively blanketing the wine with inert gas. Roughly speaking, these devices seem to be able to double the life expectancy of wine in an open bottle.

Top: The coarse art of decanting.
Bottom: The candlelight allows you to spot the sediment through the dark glass.

Combining food and wine

Food and wine have been consumed happily together for thousands of years. Why then do there seem to be such problems over wine and food partnership today? It is because we now eat and drink outside of traditional regional boundaries. Infact, our drinking and eating ranges the globe.

This has naturally forced upon us a need to experiment. The time when a handful of 'borrowed' wines could be safely drilled into duty with a similarly limited range of national dishes has long since passed. Everything is up for grabs. So what can you do to try to ensure that you notch up a good proportion of successes?

GOING NATIVE

Where drinking recommended regional wines with authentic dishes is still a possibility, do it. Why throw away the wisdom of the ages on a whim? Shellfish with Muscadet, Claret or Rioja for lamb and Sauternes with Roquefort are all classic combinations. Think about why they work and certain principles seem to emerge to help you.

BALANCING THE WEIGHT OR PRESENCE OF DISH AND WINE

One of the key principles to successful wine and food matching is to ensure that food and wine have similar weight or presence. Delicate dishes fare better with lighter wines whilst rich dishes demand something bigger. Age-old ideas such as white wine with fish and red wine with red meat generally hold true. Chicken and pork can work with both white and red, depending on how they are sauced. Red wine can work with fish, but the fish needs to be firm or richly sauced, and the wine needs to be fruity, low in tannin and high in acid, for example Bardolino or simpler Pinot Noirs.

The idea of balancing weight or presence of dish and wine will underpin all the other principles at play, and needs to be borne constantly in mind.

ACIDITY

Why is it, precisely, that crisp unoaked wines work well with shellfish and simple fish dishes? As well as our concept of weight balance, there is also the small matter of a wedge of lemon. Lemon juice added to food alters the thresholds at which our palates perceive acidity. Crisp wines with a clean-cut, even acidic, character appear softened by acidulated food; wines with less acidity seem flat – and if oaky may taste like fire-damaged cardboard. Even if your fish isn't acidulated, the fact that this is something that we do should be our guide for what style of wine to serve: a crisp, dry white mimics the way we use lemon.

Other juggling tricks with acidity

The presence of acidic elements in food is not restricted to fish. Take, for instance, sauerkraut. What do we drink with that? Riesling. Why? Because it has the necessary acidity not to be flattened by the sour cabbage.

Acid to cut fat

The other function of acidity when we put it with food is to cut fattiness. Let's consider some fatty goose or duck for a moment. You need acidity to cut the richness, but you must also balance its weight, its presence. A crisp, dry white will seem austere, aggressive, thin. The answer, if you're determinedly a white wine drinker, is to plump for a wine with some sweetness – an occasion when a German Riesling Spätlese, or Alsace Pinot Gris Vendange Tardive, say, suggest themselves. If this sounds odd, think how often we like to serve a sweet-acid fruit element with these birds; the choice of wine style begins to seem more natural.

SWEETNESS

Sweetness to match richness underpins the classic combination of foie gras with sweet wines, such as Sauternes, Jurançon Moelleux, or Sélection de Grains Nobles from Alsace. The sweetness of the sugar mirrors the soft, emollient nature of the foie; the acidity refreshes.

In more conventionally sweet contexts, the great thing is to ensure that the sweetness of the wine exceeds the sweetness of the dish – another function of perception thresholds being redefined. Balance such considerations with a judicious matching of 'weights' and you're more likely to get things right than wrong: Moscato Spumante with a strawberry and *crème pâtissière* tart; *Botrytis* Sémillon with bakewell tart; Rutherglen Muscat with sticky toffee pudding.

RED WINE AND MEAT

Red wine, at one time, was all about tannin. Nowadays a lot of wines are made with far less astringent character, as they are not designed for such long keeping. However, a bottle just off the merchant's shelf or straight from a restaurant's standard list may still not be quite ready. Is there any way to soften the mouth-puckering edge to such wines? You have two main options: decoy protein or barrier cream.

All tannin wants to do is to latch on to the nearest available soft protein. In the absence of anything else, it will settle for your gums, tongue and saliva. Unless you occupy the tannins elsewhere they will attack you. Rare meat offers a good decoy: rare steak or lamb will mop up the tannin in a young Claret or red Burgundy very nicely thank you, making the wine seem much softer and more sweetly fruited.

Soft creamy cheeses can do something similar; hard cheeses do not – all the protein is bound up with itself in long, set chains and there is none for the tannin to grab. Creamy textures also coat the palate, acting like a barrier cream against an abrasive chemical.

Conversely, softer wines such as Beaujolais, or a fruity Dolcetto, just die in the presence of available protein or creamy textures. Such tannin as they have (not a lot) is stripped out of them and the wine easily appears just gutless. These wines work better with cured meats, where the protein is all inter-combined.

Where meats are entirely cooked through – well-done roasts, casseroles and stews – choose lively, fruity wines that don't have too much tannin in them either.

HEAT

Another place to avoid excessive tannin is in the presence of foods that are noticeably peppery or chillied. At first you may rather like the extra lift that the chilli or pepper gives to the fruitiness of a wine. The effect, however, is cumulative on most people, and eventually it is the aggressive effects of tannin (and alcohol and acid, for that matter)

Fact Box

Desserts
The wine must be sweeter than the food.
Light fruit / mousse: Moscato d'Asti; German Beerenauslese
Chocolate: Banyuls; Mavrodaphne; other sweet reds
Rich: Rutherglen Muscat; Pedro Ximénez; Sweet Madeira

Guidelines on food and wine

A number of these wine and food matching principles are likely to come into play simultaneously.

Match the weight or presence of dish and wine; that way neither should overwhelm the other.

Try to imagine what fruit characteristic a wine is offering to a dish; ensure that it is the sort of fruit that you would consider putting with the food.

Fatty or rich food needs to be cut by acidity in a wine.

Where food has an acidic dimension, choose a wine with marked acidity. Unoaked is likely to work better than oaky.

Cooked-through protein (well-done meat or hard cheese) does not soften tannin; choose softer, fruity wines.

Heat from pepper or chilli accentuates both fruitiness and aggressive wine components; choose soft, ripe wines without oak and possibly also with some sweetness.

Where food has sweetness, choose a wine with even greater sweetness.

Keep a note on successful combinations and try to figure out why they worked.

that become accentuated to painful effect. Opt for soft, easy wines, even wines with a touch of sweetness. Something even quite subtle and gentle can adopt a whole new personality in the company of a hot curry.

FUSION FOODS

If anything is responsible for the breakdown of the traditional wine and food partnerships, Fusion Food is it. Its daring, inventive – even reckless – combinations of ingredients and flavours from different cultures leave the wine drinker wondering where to start. The only approach here is to do a quick 'recce' of the culinary territory, trying to ascertain what you have by way of acidity, sweetness, heat, 'available' protein etc., and crucially in what sort of relationship these elements stand to one another. The thinking goes something like

this… It's a dish with a marked chilli heat, limes, and some sweetness; it's chicken so the protein is cooked through; 'nam pla' adds a fishy, brothy element; it's quite light but quite forceful, so…? (You are bound to pause for thought.) So I need a white wine (thus avoiding unwanted interference from tannin, and marrying better with the fishy dimension), with quite high acidity (the lime), a certain sweetness (there's sweetness in the dish and sweetness is soothing with the heat) and if I were adding some fruit to the mixture, I would imagine a tropical fruit flavour, or something scented. You might then opt for a German Riesling (perhaps a Spätlese), which would have the requisite acidity, a delicate flowery character and, at the right age, a sort of tropical fruitiness. Its lack of alcohol could be helpful if the chilli is particularly hot.

Other choices might be an unoaked New World Chardonnay (but it could prove too alcoholic and leave a burn after the chilli), a New Zealand Sauvignon Blanc (but where's the sweetness? A particularly grassy or vegetal one doesn't seem to offer the right fruit) or perhaps a New World Viognier (very exotic; watch out for oak).

It's quite hard work and looks a bit more like unravelling a cryptic crossword than eating and drinking, but don't be daunted. If you're an adventurous eater anyway, trying to find the wine to match adds another dimension of fun.

CHEESEBOARDS

You may have wondered to yourself a little earlier, what you're meant to do with a cheeseboard if soft cheeses tend to do one thing and hard the opposite. Quite. A cheeseboard often presents more of a partnership problem than the old cheese and wine cliché would suggest. Much depends on the cheeseboard's composition and its position in the sequence of the meal. Some people like to finish off whatever red they are drinking (I find that many a red is indeed 'finished off' that way), whilst others like to broach the dessert wine. Another group remark, quite rightly, that crisp, dry white wines, Sauvignon Blancs especially, are just the ticket with lots of cheeses. Yes, but not strong blues, and anyway not three-quarters of the way through a dinner when they will taste thin and tart after a full red.

A good approach is to keep the red on the table, if that's what people want, and to serve a semi-sweet wine as a bridging option to dessert wine. Thinking fruit accompaniment is helpful. Apples, grapes, dried raisins and figs all come to mind as adornments to the cheeseboard. Their wine equivalents work similarly: sweet Chenin Blanc (apples), Muscat (grapes!) and also Italian passito wines (raisins and dried figs).

CONCLUSION

You're not always going to get it bang on right – probably nobody does. But with a little thought you are going to avoid any huge disasters and are no doubt going to have a jolly good time. Try to keep a mental, or, better still, a written note of any happy food and wine combinations and try to figure out how and why they worked so well. You'll need to think about all the elements in a dish. With any luck you'll end up with a large repertoire of surefire winning combinations to dip into again and again, and from which you'll also be able to strike out further.

Cheese and wine. Not always a marriage made in heaven.

What can go wrong with wine

Given that wine is a food substance, it is not surprising that there are parallels between what can go wrong with food and what can go wrong with wine. That said, the alcohol in wine, and its high acidity, make it a pretty hostile environment for most of the bugs that cause food poisoning.

Commonly encountered wine faults
Oxidation

No wine is immortal, and it is air contact that will eventually push all wines over the hill. Oxygen is the most reactive part of the atmosphere, and where it attacks a wine the result is oxidation. When wine starts to oxidise the first thing you tend to notice is a loss of freshness and fruit aromas. With more extreme oxidation the colour of the wine goes brown and the wine takes on a 'sherry-like' smell (most styles of Sherry are oxidised on purpose – *see page 135*). If too much air comes into contact with wine during the maturation or the bottling then a whole consignment of wine can oxidise. By contrast, a porous cork can cause a single bottle to oxidise whilst the rest of the batch is in perfect condition. It is oxidation that limits the life of a wine once the bottle has been opened (*see page 21*).

Secondary fermentation (re-fermentation)

There is always a risk with a medium or sweet wine that rogue yeast might start the wine fermenting again. The wine will go cloudy, start to smell a bit like scrumpy cider and turn fizzy. The pressure from the carbon dioxide can force the corks out of bottles, or in some cases, particularly with screw-top closures, cause the bottles to explode. Alcohol inhibits secondary fermentation, so the higher the alcohol content in the wine the less likely it is to re-ferment. This is why secondary fermentation is more likely in a German wine at 8%ABV than a Sauternes at 14%ABV.

Volatility

One of the strains of bacteria that can flourish in wine is *Acetobacter*. If wine or grape juice is attacked by this bacterium in the presence of air then acetic acid will be formed. Acetic acid is what gives vinegar its pungent, volatile smell. For this reason winemakers often refer to acetic acid as 'volatile acidity' (or just 'VA'). Volatile wine is often slightly cloudy, with a suspension at its surface. There is sometimes a distinct vinegary smell to the wine. However, very often the acetic acid reacts with the alcohol to produce a compound called ethyl acetate. This substance has an extraordinary aroma rather like the smell of nail varnish remover. Glue sniffers will feel very much at home with this sort of wine.

Cork taint

'Waiter, this wine is corked' is as much of a cliché as 'Waiter, there's a fly in my soup'. The sad reality is that most consumers and restaurant or bar staff do not know how to spot a corked wine in the first place. Most wine returned as 'corked' is either perfectly sound, or it is suffering from one of the other faults, such as oxidation. In fact, I am sure that most genuinely corked wine is drunk without complaint.

For a start, cork taint is nothing to do with having fragments of cork floating around in the glass. Such fragments of cork, or cork dust, may be unsightly, but they will not affect the flavour of the wine. One of the reasons why 'cork taint' is so often mis-diagnosed is that the wine and the cork look fine. The telltale signature of cork taint is a mouldy, fungal, 'damp curtains' smell on the nose.

Wines vary in their degree of corkiness, so whilst some reek of the taint, others have just a hint of flatness and dustiness on the nose. However, once the wine is in your mouth any traces of cork taint will tend to become more pronounced. Estimates of the incidence of cork taint vary, but

something like 2–5% of all natural corks at the moment seem to taint their wines to some degree. The whole debate about cork taint, and the alternatives to natural cork, has become very heated of late (*see page 56*).

Tartrate crystals

These are not really a fault at all, but in some markets it is very difficult to sell wine with a crystalline deposit. The main acid present in grapes and wine is tartaric acid. This acid usually goes through the whole winemaking process unchanged, giving the finished wine much of its refreshing crispness. However, what happens sometimes is that the salts of tartaric acid

Spotting faulted wines. The wine on the left is oxidising. The middle one was corked on the nose. The cloudiness of the right suggests that a secondary fermentation is taking place.

Fact Box

Common wine faults

Oxidation.
Secondary fermentation.
Volatility.
Cork taint.
(Tartrate crystals).
Foreign bodies.

precipitate in the bottle, forming 'tartrate crystals'. Although the crystals are perfectly harmless, and have no effect on the quality or the flavour of the wine, they seem to provoke paranoia and hysteria in some consumers. Letters are dispatched to MPs and Environmental Health Officers. If you do not like the look of the crystals, just carefully decant the wine. Some winemakers try to minimise the risk of tartrate crystal formation by cold treating their wines before bottling (*see page 56*).

Foreign bodies

You may come across the odd insect or spider that met a glorious end drowning in a bottle of wine. However, most modern bottling facilities are clean and hygienic, so such protein supplements in wine are an infrequent occurrence nowadays. What does worry producers even today is the occasional incidence of glass fragments in bottles. The problem rarely now arises during the manufacture of the bottles. Rather, the fragments are often caused by the filling machine just chipping the edge of the necks of the bottles. If you ever spot what look like shards of glass in a bottle

Don't panic. These are the harmless tartrate crystals that form in many wines.

of wine, do contact the retailer of the wine as quickly as possible. It is in everyone's interest to get the wine recalled if there is a risk to health.

If you think that the wine you have purchased is suffering from one of these faults, it is worth requesting either a refund or a replacement from the establishment that sold you the wine. Keep the out-of-condition wine so that the retailer can check for themselves what the problem is. However, you cannot blame retailers for being sceptical when a bottle of wine is returned as faulted when there is only a teaspoon of wine left in the bottom of the bottle.

WHAT CAN GO WRONG WITH YOU

Everyone who reads this is going to die at some point. No matter how we eat, drink, exercise or fornicate, our days on this earth are numbered. If you are worried, talk to your doctor. You might also want to read Dr. Tom Stuttaford's excellent book (*for details see page 186*) about drink and health. If you are still really worried about your mortality, talk to a priest.

Prolonged heavy drinking, and one-off binge drinking, can accelerate your demise. Ischaemic and haemorrhagic stroke, lethal arrhythmia, alcoholic cardiomyopathy, liver cirrhosis, alcoholic hepatitis and alcoholic dementia can all be caused, to a greater or lesser degree, by over-indulgence. As well as destroying themselves, those who drink to excess risk bringing social, emotional and financial distress to their family, friends and colleagues. The potential dangers of drinking too much may be so scary that you may choose to abstain.

The beneficial side to alcohol

However (and it's a very big 'however'), there is another side to alcohol and health. Light to moderate drinking (2–4 units of alcohol per day) exposes the average imbiber to few if any of the disastrous problems associated with heavy drinking. What is more, there is a growing corpus of research, building on millennia of anecdotal observation, that sensible drinking can have positive health benefits. Epidemiological studies have shown that the death rate, not just from heart disease, but from all causes, is lower amongst light and moderate drinkers that it is amongst tee-totallers and heavy drinkers.

Why alcohol in moderation is beneficial to human health is gradually being elucidated. Part of the positive effect on cardiovascular disease is probably related to the effect of alcohol on the levels and the balance of blood lipoproteins. All types of alcoholic drink can bring about these beneficial changes. Interestingly though, some of the positive attributes of different drinks may be linked not just to alcohol but also to other trace compounds present in the brew. This may be the reason why red wine in particular seems to have a beneficial action.

Detailed medical issues aside, perhaps the most sensible approach to wine and health is to read Hugh Johnson's or Tim Unwin's books (*see page 186*) about the history of wine. Wine has been intimately tied in with Western Civilisation since as far back as our written and most of our archaeological records go. We have got to where we are today without having been destroyed by booze. Why should the experience of our generation and future ones be so different?

And finally...
The pleasure to be derived from drinking wine with good food and in pleasant company goes a long way towards making our lives worth living.

Making wine

Grape growing

The production of wine can be divided neatly between the growing of the grapes (viticulture) and the turning of those grapes into wine (vinification). Although grape growing and winemaking are separate disciplines, the crafting of truly great wine requires excellence in both the vineyard and winery.

The European Union (EU) definition of wine is as follows: 'Wine is the product obtained from the total or partial alcoholic fermentation of fresh grapes, whether or not crushed, or of grape must.'

The scariest part of making wine is the growing of the grapes. A vineyard on a summer's day might seem idyllic, but returning to prune the vines in winter can feel like banishment to a gulag.

Grapes are just like any other crop in that the growth of the vine, and the quality of the fruit it produces, are influenced by both Nature and Man. These influences can be divided into four natural factors – climate, weather, soil, aspect – over which we have little control, and four human factors – grape variety, vine age, pruning and training, caring for the vines – where knowledge, skill and money can be brought to bear. The principal grape varieties, and their clones, merit a section to themselves; here we look at all the other aspects of grape growing.

CLIMATE

Climate can be thought of as the single most important factor in grape growing. Without the right climate grape growing is virtually impossible. Vines require a temperate climate, with winter temperatures low enough to keep the vines dormant, and summer temperatures high enough to ripen the grapes. This sort of climate occurs in two bands of latitude on the Earth's surface, 30–50° North and 30–50° South. As well as being found in these two zones, most of the world's vineyards are reasonably close to a large expanse of water, be it ocean, sea or a large lake. The water will tend to moderate the possible extremes of temperature. What is more, it is the weather systems coming off the oceans that provide the rainfall to sustain viticulture in many parts of the world. That said, whilst most vineyards in Europe rely on natural rainfall for their water, in the New World many vineyards are equipped with irrigation systems.

Within the zones where vineyards are found, climate has a big influence on the types of wine that any area can produce. This is a result of the way the climate influences the ripening of the grapes. In a cool climate area, such as in the Mosel Valley in Germany, the whole ripening process is slow. In other words, the build-up of sugar in the grapes during the summer and autumn is very gradual, as is the drop in acidity. Even if the grapes are not picked until late October, their sugar levels will still be quite modest. This will translate into modest alcohol levels in the finished wine (many Mosel wines are only 8% alcohol by volume, ABV). Because fresh acidity

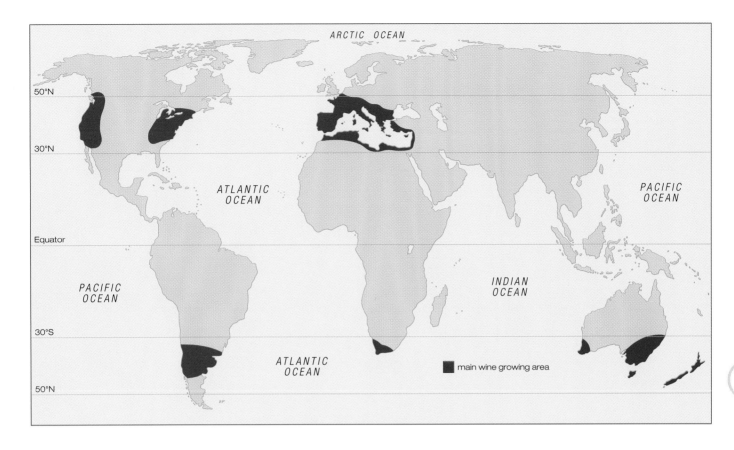

is part of the character of many fine still and sparkling white wines, cool climate areas often focus on white wine production.

In a warm climate area, such as the Rhône Valley in France, the whole ripening process is much quicker. Even though the grapes will be picked much earlier than in a cool climate area, the warm climate grapes will contain a larger amount of sugar and this will then translate into some heroic alcohol levels. It is not unusual to find Rhône wines like Châteauneuf-du-Pape with 14%ABV. However, the flip side is that such wines will tend to be relatively low in acidity.

Although there are numerous exceptions, one can probably just about get away with saying that the warmer climate areas are better suited to producing red wine.

WEATHER

The weather will always be the great variable in wine. We can control most things in the vineyard and winery nowadays, but not the weather. The weather will have a bearing on the size of the harvest each year, but perhaps even more crucially, it will define the quality of the grapes. There is a maxim that 'You can make poor wine from good grapes, but it is impossible to make good wine from poor grapes'. The importance of the weather is emphasised in the way that most wines carry a vintage (harvest) date on their labels. Because of the variation of weather from one year to the next we have the whole idea of 'good vintages' and 'bad vintages'. These generalised results for the world's main wine regions are often summarised in vintage charts.

Most of the world's vineyards lie between 30° and 50° North and between 30° and 50° South.

Outlined below is what might be thought of as a perfect year's vineyard weather. The indicated months refer to the northern hemisphere (just count forward six months for the equivalent in the southern hemisphere).

Winter (November–February)

This is the vine's dormant period. A couple of weeks of really cold weather in December or January is good news as it kills off a lot of overwintering pests. The cold also helps to keep the vine safely in its dormant state. Heavy rainfall in the winter is important as it restores soil moisture levels. Drought problems can develop in the summer if there was insufficient winter rain. The grower's main job in the winter (particularly February) is pruning the vines.

An homage to Vivaldi. The four seasons in Champagne.

Spring (March–May)

Bud burst takes place in March. Warm, mild weather is desirable. In the later part of the spring the vine puts on a major spurt of growth, so some rain does no harm.

Summer (June–August)

The vines flower in June. Fine, dry weather is important for a successful flowering. Assuming the flowering has gone well, by the end of June the immature bunches of grapes will have started to form. If the crop looks as if it will be excessive, some quality-conscious estates will crop thin at this stage (known in French as *vendange verte* or *éclaircissage*). By the early summer the vine's vegetation will be pretty rampant, so a lot of trimming and tying up of the shoots takes place. Some spraying will usually also be necessary (*see page 40*). Hot, dry and sunny conditions are needed in July and August to power the development of the grapes. Up until the beginning of August all grape varieties are green in colour. The colour forms in the skin of black grapes over a period of a few days early in August, a process known as 'véraison'.

Autumn (September–October)

September is the crucial month for determining the ultimate quality of a wine. The odd shower at the very start of the month can relieve any water stress that has built up during the summer months. All that is then needed are four or five weeks of dry, ideally sunny weather, so that the vines can complete the ripening of the grapes, and the picking can take place. From the flowering at the beginning of June to the harvest in September is approximately 100 days.

Many vineyards are still hand harvested. This is a slow, laborious and expensive business, but the advantage is that the grapes can be carefully selected and sorted (*triage*). Increasingly though,

vineyards are now being adapted for machine picking. These picking machines are very quick and cheap to operate, with a huge saving coming from not having to pay, feed and accommodate a large team of pickers. However, machine-picked grapes cannot be as carefully sorted as hand-picked fruit. Where there can be a distinct advantage to machine picking is in warm climate areas. Harvesting machines can pick in the cool of the night, thus preserving the freshness and acidity of the fruit.

SOIL

The influence of soil on quality and style remains the single most controversial issue about wine. The one thing everyone does agree on is that vines need to be planted in soils that drain well. Beyond that, things get trickier.

In France, the soil is central to the concept of *terroir*. The word *terroir* in the context of wine is hard to translate into English, but one can think of it as the 'vine's environment'. As well as soil, other elements of the *terroir* include aspect (*see below*) and microclimate (the climate in any particular field, as opposed to a region as a whole). For most grape growers in France it is the *terroir*, and in particular the soil, that is the origin of the variation of quality and style between vineyards and regions. Probably the most drastic manifestation of the cult of *terroir* is in Burgundy, where each individual field is thought of as having its own unique *terroir*. Many of the 'best' *terroirs* in France actually have very poor, often stony, soils. These soils limit the vine's vigour, naturally restricting the yield but in so doing force the plant to direct its energy into ripening the fruit.

In the past it was probably fair to say that the further one travelled from France the less central the role of soil was seen to be in determining the

Serious *terroir*. The granite soil found in many of the finest Beaujolais vineyards.

quality of a wine. However, areas of the New World, such as Coonawarra in Australia, are now regarded as having their unique *terroirs*, which define the style of wine produced there.

ASPECT

It is no coincidence that in many of Europe's cool climate regions the vineyards are found on south-facing slopes (e.g. the small Rheingau region in Germany). In addition to providing better sun exposure, sloping sites tend to have well-drained soils. They may well be sheltered from the cold northerly winds and there is also some natural frost protection as the cold air sinks to the bottom of a slope. The rub with steeply sloping vineyards is the cost of cultivation. Particularly in the case of terraced vineyards nearly all the work will have to be done by hand.

Grape growing

VINE AGE

It can take a newly planted vine cutting three or four years before it produces its first crop of grapes. Once cropping, a young vine will produce a sizeable yield for about 25 years. The rub is that the quality of the fruit is nothing special. Once past its 30th birthday the concentration of the fruit increases, but the yield declines. This is the reason why many of the world's finest wines are made from old vines. Equally, it is part of the reason, given the low-yielding nature of old vines, why these wines are so expensive. The average vine age at Château Latour, for instance, is around 60 years old. Old vines are not just an Old World phenomenon. Henschke in Australia have some vines in the Hill of Grace vineyard that were planted in the 1860s.

The luxury of having old vines is all well and good if you are producing wines that can command a vast price. However, for normal wine production young high-yielding vines are what is required. Hence most vineyards are re-planted every 30 years or so.

PRUNING AND TRAINING

Without pruning and training the vine would over-crop, the vineyard would become unmanageable, and grape quality would suffer. By pruning the vine the yield in the coming season is cut. This forces the vine to direct its ripening efforts into a smaller number of grapes, so improving their concentration. The most important month for pruning in the northern hemisphere is February. Training the vine along wires or up a post keeps the vineyard neat, making it much easier to get around the vineyard for spraying, trimming and harvesting. Training is also important for maximising the exposure of the leaves to the sun, essential for the production of sugar and therefore the ripening of the grapes.

Not surprisingly, over the centuries growers in different parts of the world have developed pruning and training systems to suit their local conditions. That said, all of them are variations on two basic approaches, cane pruning and spur pruning (see opposite). The variety of grape planted will be a huge influence on which style of pruning is selected.

Most of Europe's classic vineyards are densely planted with vines. In Burgundy there are often 10,000 vines per hectare, with only one metre between each row of vines. There are numerous

Far right: Two different training systems being used in adjoining plots in Burgundy.
Below: A Bradman amongst vines. One of the Shiraz centurions in Henschke's Hill of Grace vineyard.

arguments about how this can be advantageous, not least in limiting each vine's vigour through root competition. However, problems arise when you want to mechanise such a vineyard. Specially adapted tractors have to be used. In most parts of the New World the vines are planted at a much lower density, allowing a normal tractor to negotiate the vineyard. With a lower vine density, most individual vines in the New World are much bigger.

CARING FOR THE VINES

Like any type of farming, there are various threats to the vine's health and particularly its ability to produce high-quality grapes. These scourges fall into four groups: weather problems, soil problems, pests and diseases. Some of these challenges can be combated by the grower, whereas with others it is down to good old-fashioned prayer power.

Weather problems

Winter frost During the winter dormant period the vine can cope with snow and any 'normal' cold snaps. However, if the temperature suddenly plummets below -16°C (3°F) then the vine will freeze and die. The only response is to dig up the dead vine and re-plant from scratch. The grower will have to wait several years before the new vine is cropping, and perhaps a generation before the quality of fruit is back to where it was before the mature vine was killed. The good news is that winter frost is a relatively rare problem, not least because vineyards are not planted in regions where this sort of severe cold is an annual occurrence. One way to offer the vine some protection is to plough the earth over the base of the vine. The soil then acts as an insulating blanket.

Spring frost A more frequent problem for many growers is spring frost. As already mentioned,

More about pruning

Cane pruning The simplest version of cane pruning is called *Guyot Simple*. The vine is cut back to the old wood, except for one cane from the previous year (a cane will usually have about six buds on it). This cane is trained horizontally along a wire. In the spring the buds on the cane open, producing the shoots, leaves and flowers. After the harvest in the autumn the leaves fall and the shoots harden into canes. From these canes the pruner will select the cane for the following year. Where two canes are retained the system is called *Guyot Double*.

Spur pruning Bush training is the simplest type of spur pruning. The vine is pruned back to the old wood, except this time several 'arms' are retained, each of which has at its end a short spur of last year's wood (a spur will often have only two or three buds on it). The buds open, producing the shoots, leaves and flowers. With a bush vine there is no support for the shoots, so the growth will often sprawl. After the harvest the shoots will harden into canes. Come the winter the pruner will cut these canes back, leaving a short spur at the end of each arm. In some cases, to neaten up a spur pruned vine the shoots will be tied to a stake driven into the soil just next to the vine. This is referred to as *Gobelet* training. If by contrast the old wood is trained along a wire, spreading the spurs out horizontally, then you have *Cordon* training.

whilst the vine is dormant it is quite frost tolerant. However, the new shoots emerging in the spring-time are extremely sensitive to even a minor frost, -1°C (30°F). The embryonic flower is present on the shoot, so if it is killed there will be a loss of crop. However, the vine as a whole will survive through producing secondary shoots and leaves. There are several ways of limiting spring frost damage. One approach is to place heaters or burners at regular intervals throughout a vineyard, in the hope of keeping the temperature at vine

Oil-burning smoke pots used to limit spring frost damage in Chablis.

level just above freezing point. In addition, fans can be installed to keep the air circulating, pre-venting cold, still air from settling on the vines. The most ingenious technique is to spray the vines with water all night long (a process called 'asper-sion'). When the temperature reaches 0°C (32°F) the water droplets on the vine shoots will start to freeze. However, the latent heat released as this happens prevents the shoots themselves from suffering any injury. The following morning the vine is caked in ice, but when this melts away the tender growth emerges undamaged.

Unsettled weather at flowering The success or failure of the flowering is very dependent on the weather at that particular time. A period of cool weather just before the flowering (or perversely a sudden hot spell) can cause some of the tiny grapes to drop off. This phenomenon is called 'coulure'. Poor weather, particularly rainfall, actually during the flowering stage leads to a failure of pollination. 'Millerandage', as it is called, results in bunches of grapes that contain both full-sized berries and a number of small, 'runt' berries. The net effect of both coulure and millerandage is to get a smaller harvest than normal.

Drought A hot dry summer, particularly if it follows a dry winter, can lead to the vine suffering from water stress. The whole ripening process will actually stop. In France this summer shutdown is usually relieved by rainfall at the end of August or the beginning of September, but in most parts of the New World the ripening process is kept on track by the use of irrigation systems.

Hail In five minutes a hailstorm can completely wipe out a year's crop. The hailstones will strip the leaves off the vine and batter the grapes to the ground. Even if the grapes stay on the vine, the damage caused by the hailstones will allow fungal diseases to develop on the skin and then the fruit will be destroyed. The one consolation is that hail is usually a very localised problem. One vineyard may be hit, but a plot a couple of kilometres away may be completely unaffected. By firing rockets into the thunderclouds (I'm serious) that bring the hailstones, some growers hope that the moisture will fall as water rather than ice.

Rain at harvest Heavy rainfall just before or during the harvest can badly compromise the quality of the grapes. The vine will soak up the moisture and use it to swell up the grapes. All the grape's constituents become diluted: sugar, acid and also flavour. The producer will end up with more wine, but with a concomitant loss of concentration. If it is both warm and wet then things can get even worse. High humidity helps to trigger the appearance of Grey Rot (*see page 40*).

Soil problems

Grape growing being a monoculture, nutrient deficiencies will eventually arise in most vineyards. Perhaps the most famous example of this is where an iron deficiency causes the premature yellowing of the vine's leaves ('chlorosis'). One solution to this sort of problem is to have the soil analysed, then apply an appropriate fertiliser. Whilst a short-term problem can be corrected in this way, growers have now come to realise that the excessive use of synthetic fertilisers can destroy the soil structure, and alter the natural balance of the flora and fauna. This is part of the reason why there has been an increasing interest in a return to 'organic viticulture'. The soil is kept healthy and balanced through the use of manure, compost and cover crops. An even more radical alternative is 'biodynamic viticulture'. In this case not only are synthetic vineyard treatments shunned, but the timing of the vineyard work is controlled by reference to the moon and stars.

Pests

The list of creatures that will munch vines and grapes is daunting. Amongst the mammals, kangaroos, rabbits and baboons all enjoy the odd bunch. Many species of bird are not averse to eating grapes either. Apart from the obvious solution of shooting the unwanted visitors, various scaring devices and netting are also employed in some vineyards.

Invertebrate pests include various caterpillars, leaf hoppers and mites. These can be controlled by pesticide sprays. However, a lot of work is also going into the use of biological control.

Phylloxera The greatest challenge to the vine has come from a tiny aphid called *Phylloxera vastatrix* (the vine louse). *Phylloxera* attacks the roots of the *Vitis vinifera* vine, eventually destroying the root system and killing the vine. *Phylloxera* was inadvertently spread around most of the world's vineyards in the second half of the nineteenth century, before people realised the huge devastation it could cause. Within three or four years growers saw healthy, productive vineyards annihilated. Various sprays and other techniques for combating the *Phylloxera* louse were proposed, but it is virtually impossible to kill something that is living deep down in the soil.

The solution came through the observation that many of the American vine species (*Vitis rupestris, Vitis riparia* and *Vitis berlandieri*) are resistant to *Phylloxera*. This is not surprising as we now know that *Phylloxera* originated on the East Coast of the USA. One option was to plant vineyards with American vines, or hybrid vines (*Vitis vinifera* x American vine, *see page 49*). However, the quality of wines produced from such vines is not brilliant. The answer was to grow up an American vine, and to then graft a *Vitis vinifera* on to it. When planted out in the vineyards the American rootstock provides the *Phylloxera* resistance, whereas the *Vitis vinifera* scion produces the quality fruit. Most of the world's vineyards are now planted with vines that are grafted in this way. There is a huge range of different rootstocks available to suit different soil types and other growing conditions.

A few vineyard regions have managed to stay free of *Phylloxera*. In these circumstances the *Vitis vinifera* vines can still be planted on their own roots. Chile, Cyprus and South Australia have all managed to keep *Phylloxera* out of their vineyards. In the past this was through geographical isolation and good fortune. Nowadays, strict quarantine rules apply.

Phylloxera does not cope very well with extremely sandy soils. Hence the vineyards in Colares in Portugal have managed to stay ungrafted because they are sited on sand dunes.

Isolation and sandy soils apart, there are a few freak plots of vines in *Phylloxera*-infested regions that have never succumbed to this vine louse. Bollinger in Champagne is one example. They own a couple of small vineyards that have never been grafted (these grapes are used to make Bollinger Vieilles Vignes Françaises). Another example is in the Douro region in Portugal, where Quinta do Noval Nacional is similarly made from a plot of ungrafted vines.

Being able to plant vines on their own roots saves growers a fortune in grafting costs. Ungrafted vines also tend to live longer than grafted vines.

Nematodes There is another group of soil pests called Nematodes. These are microscopic worms that attack the vine roots. As well as causing direct root damage, some species have also been shown to spread viral diseases. To combat this problem, a number of specially developed Nematode-resistant rootstocks can be used in heavily infested soils.

Diseases

Fungal diseases are a big threat in many of the world's vineyards. In the spring and early summer the main challenge is posed by two versions of mildew. Downy Mildew (also called *Peronospera*) and Powdery Mildew (also called *Oidium*) attack the tender growth of the vine. If unchecked, the yield and quality of the crops can be very badly affected. However, the good news is that two simple preventative sprays are available to the grower. Bordeaux mixture (copper sulphate, lime and water) can be deployed against Downy Mildew. Powdery Mildew can be prevented by dusting the vine with powdered sulphur.

Botrytis Later in the summer and in the run up to the harvest, the big worry is Grey Rot. This disease is caused by a fungus called *Botrytis cinerea*. Grey Rot attacks the bunch of grapes. It destroys the grape skin and renders the fruit totally unfit for winemaking. Humidity, hail damage and excessively thick leaf growth can all contribute to an outbreak of Grey Rot. Fungicide sprays are available, but *Botrytis* has a habit of quickly developing a resistance to the various treatments.

There is a redeeming side to *Botrytis cinerea*. In some vineyard regions the harvest of fully ripe white grapes will be delayed by a couple of weeks or more. If the autumn weather stays fine, ideally with some early morning mist and warmth in the afternoon, then the *Botrytis* will cause Noble Rot (in French this is called *Pourriture Noble*; in German it is called *Edelfäule*). In this case the affected berries will gradually shrivel up into what look like dark grey raisins. When picked and pressed these berries will yield a lusciously sweet juice, the basis of many of the world's finest sweet white wines (e.g. Sauternes, Barsac, Coteaux du Layon, Sélection de Grains Nobles, Tokaji Aszú and Trockenbeerenauslese).

Making wine from grapes with Noble Rot is risky and expensive. Firstly, without the right sort of autumn weather, the Noble Rot will not appear. Secondly, it is usually necessary to pick the Noble Rot berries one at a time, as the whole bunch is not affected uniformly. This may involve the pickers in a number of passages through the vineyard ('tris') over a long period. Thirdly, when the desiccated Noble Rot berries come to be pressed, only a small amount of juice oozes out.

Other fungal diseases include Anthracnose, Black Rot and Eutypiose. The latter is spread through pruning wounds and is a big worry in the Cognac region.

Viral and bacterial diseases In recent years a lot of research work has gone into understanding the viral diseases that affect the vines. Although vine viruses rarely kill the plant outright, they cause a progressive diminution of yield and can delay the ripening of the grapes. Leaf-roll Virus and Fan-leaf Virus are two examples. Tissue culture techniques are now being employed to try to produce virus-free nursery material.

Bacterial diseases, such as Pierce's Disease, and Phytoplasma diseases, such as Grapevine Yellows, are now a growing concern in some parts of the world. Growers in California are particularly worried by the rapid spread of Pierce's Disease.

Doomed to die. *Phylloxera-infected vines in California.*

Grape varieties

Several species of vine exist in nature, but most wine is made from just one species, *Vitis vinifera*. There are over 1000 different varieties of *Vitis vinifera* in existence, each making wines that smell and taste different. Out of this enormous line-up there are around 20 that nowadays form an international 'jet set'.

CHARDONNAY

Home patch: France (Burgundy, Champagne).

Successes elsewhere: Everywhere? Being tough: New Zealand (Marlborough), Australia (Margaret River, Adelaide Hills), California (Carneros, Santa Maria Valley). Some cheaper decent efforts: France (Languedoc), Italy (Trentino, Puglia), South Africa, Chile (Casablanca Valley).

Aromas: In warm climates: mango, melon, pineapple. In cooler climates they are more restrained and 'green'. A lot of the aromas associated with Chardonnay result from the way it is fermented and matured (*see page 53*): butter, cream, toast, biscuit.

Main wine styles: The dominant style of Chardonnay world-wide developed from white Burgundies such as Meursault. These wines are often full in colour, have ripe fruit overlaid with oak and other complex notes, and on the palate they are rich but dry.

The other school of Chardonnay also has its origins in the French region of Burgundy, but in the village of Chablis. This style is more austere, there is little or no oak, the colour is usually paler and the backbone of acidity is much more pronounced. Chardonnay is also an important, and very often the sole, component of many of the world's finest sparkling wines.

SAUVIGNON BLANC (FUME BLANC)

Home patch: France (Central Vineyards, Bordeaux).

Successes elsewhere: New Zealand (Marlborough), Chile (Casablanca Valley), California (Napa Valley).

Aromas: Everything green: grass, leaves, gooseberry, green apple, pear, asparagus.

Main wine styles: Sauvignon Blanc is best known for its pale coloured, powerfully fruity, dry and crisply acid white wines. In the Napa Valley (and at the top level in Bordeaux – usually in conjunction with Sémillon) a riper, fuller, oak-aged style of Sauvignon is produced (sometimes labelled as 'Fumé Blanc').

RIESLING

Home patch: Germany (Mosel-Saar-Ruwer, Rheingau), France (Alsace).

Successes elsewhere: Austria, Australia.

Aromas: When young: apple, lime and other citrus fruits, floral. With bottle age: diesel, nuts.

Main wine styles: At one extreme Riesling can be bone dry, with an austere, minerally fruit character. At the other end of the scale it produces the world's finest and most harmonious sweet white wines. In between are delicate, poised, medium white wines. Whatever the style, all Rieslings have high underlying acidity.

SEMILLON

Home patch: France (Bordeaux).

Successes elsewhere: Australia.

Aromas: Often broad and oily, some green fruits. With Noble Rot: honeyed and rich.

Main wine styles: In Australia a lot of Sémillon is cropped heavily to produce an inexpensive, broad, clean blending partner for Chardonnay. With care it produces a dry white wine, which though austere when young, can develop some complexity in the bottle. Sémillon can also take to oak well if the latter is used judiciously. Sémillon in Bordeaux often produces rather simple, if not unpleasant wines, such as Entre-Deux-Mers. Sauvignon Blanc will usually be blended in to give some aromatic lift. Again though, with care and oak some impressive dry white wines can be produced.

What really takes Sémillon to another plane though is Noble Rot. Sémillon has a thin skin that makes it prone to Noble Rot, and therefore capable of making great sweet wines such as Sauternes.

CHENIN BLANC

Home patch: Loire (Anjou-Saumur, Touraine).

Successes elsewhere: South Africa.

Aromas: Sharp, sour green fruits (especially cooking apple), damp wool.

Main wine styles: Chenin Blanc has the same sort of versatility as Riesling. The dry versions, particularly in South Africa, can be rather neutral. However, in the Loire region of France, the best dry Savennières and Vouvrays can be very characterful. A lot of dull, medium dry Chenin Blanc wine is produced. However, when attacked by Noble Rot, Chenin Blanc can become something really quite special. This grape variety is also used as a base for the Loire's sparkling wines, for example Saumur.

Top: Chardonnay.
Centre: Riesling.
Bottom: Sauvignon Blanc.

MUSCAT (MOSCATO, MOSCATEL)

Home patch: The Mediterranean.

Successes elsewhere: France (Alsace), Australia (Rutherglen).

Aromas: When young: grape, peach, floral. With wood ageing: rich, opulent, raisin.

Main wine styles: It is extremely hard to generalise about Muscat because there are several distinct grape varieties that share the name. That said, the dry styles of Muscat, such as those produced in Alsace, tend to be pale in colour, with an exaggerated floral nose, and a moderate to low acidity content on the palate.

At the other extreme there are the fortified sweet Muscats. These wines can be youthful and peachy, for example Muscat de Beaumes de Venise, or dark, rich and raisiny, such as Rutherglen. Muscat is also responsible for medium sweet sparkling wines like Asti.

GEWURZTRAMINER

Home patch: France (Alsace), Italy (Trentino).

Successes elsewhere: Patchy elsewhere, with some successes in New Zealand.

Aromas: Intensely aromatic, tropical fruits (especially lychee), floral (rose, hyacinth), spicy (*Gewürz* is the German word for 'spicy').

Main wine styles: A classic Alsace Gewurztraminer is deeply coloured and hugely aromatic on the nose. For a white wine, it is full and rich on the palate with relatively low acidity and is also often just off-dry.

Late-harvested wines can be even more intense on the nose and distinctly sweet on the palate. Most Gewürztraminer wines from outside Alsace tend to be less pungent and are lighter on the palate.

Top: Muscat.
Centre: Cabernet Sauvignon.
Bottom: Merlot.

MULLER-THURGAU (RIVANER)

Home patch: Germany (Rheinhessen, Pfalz).

Successes elsewhere: England, Luxembourg, New Zealand.

Aromas: Floral (elderflower), sharp fruits.

Main wine styles: Müller-Thurgau produces medium dry or dry white wines, which are usually simple, floral and inexpensive.

PINOT GRIS
(PINOT GRIGIO, RULANDER)

Home patch: France (Alsace), Italy (Trentino, Friuli).

Successes elsewhere: Germany, just starting to gain momentum in the New World.

Aromas: Oily, broad, nutty, some white fruits.

Main wine styles: In Alsace Pinot Gris can produce wines that are quite full and rich on the palate, without being obviously aromatic on the nose. The wines are usually dry or off-dry, with good underpinning acidity.

The Pinot Grigio in Italy produces wines that are much lighter bodied and bone dry, usually having decent acidity. On the nose they are clean and neutral.

VIOGNIER

Home patch: France (Rhône).

Successes elsewhere: France (Languedoc), Australia, Argentina, California.

Aromas: Rich and exotic, peach, apricot.

Main wine styles: A top-flight Viognier will have quite a deep golden colour and an intense exotic aroma. The palate is rich and opulent, with high alcohol and low acidity. Some oak nuances may also be present, but these should never overwhelm the hedonistic fruit. There is always a touch of decadence about really good Viognier.

CABERNET SAUVIGNON

Home patch: France (Bordeaux).

Successes elsewhere: How long have you got?

Being tough: Italy (Tuscany), Australia (Coonawarra, Margaret River), South Africa (Stellenbosch), Chile (Aconcagua, Maipo, Rapel), California (Napa, Sonoma). Some decent efforts: France (Languedoc), Bulgaria, New Zealand (Hawkes Bay).

Aromas: When young: blackcurrant, liqueur de cassis, mint, stalky. With age: tobacco, dry leaves, bonfire, cedar.

Main wine styles: Top-flight Cabernet Sauvignons when young are opaque in colour, often showing a restrained dark fruit character on the nose. There is usually a good blast of new oak as well. The palate structure can be brutal, with dense fruit and chewy tannins (accentuated by decent acidity in many cases). With bottle age the rough edges are smoothed off and a fantastically complex bouquet develops. Lesser Cabernet Sauvignons are looser knit, and can be a bit green and stalky.

MERLOT

Home patch: France (Bordeaux).

Successes elsewhere: California (Napa, Sonoma), Washington State, Chile, South Africa.

Aromas: Blackberry, plum, herbal, chocolate.

Main wine styles: Like its Bordeaux sibling, young Merlot is usually deeply coloured. The nose is more open and immediately beguiling, with a different spectrum of fruit aromas. Whilst often fuller and more opulent than Cabernet on the palate, the Merlot will have less acidity and softer tannins. Being less tough to start with, Merlots come around more quickly in the bottle, developing a herbal complexity. Cheaper Merlots can be diffuse with a stewed fruit character.

PINOT NOIR

Home patch: France (Burgundy, Champagne).

Successes elsewhere: Patchy: Oregon, California (Carneros), South Africa (Walker Bay), Australia (Victoria), New Zealand (Martinborough).

Aromas: When young: red cherry, raspberry, red-currant. With age: vegetal, hessian, manure.

Main wine styles: Pinot Noir produces the world's most elegant red wines. Being a lightly pigmented grape, these wines are relatively pale in colour. The hue on the rim of Pinots fades to garnet and brick after a short time in the bottle. The cool red fruit character of young Pinot Noir is unforgettable. As Pinot matures, complex 'animal' smells develop. Although never full-bodied, Pinots can surprise the unwary with their grip on the palate. Poorly made Pinot can be wretched. In Champagne, Pinot Noir is often the backbone of the blend.

SYRAH (SHIRAZ)

Home patch: France (Rhône).

Successes elsewhere: Australia (Barossa, McClaren Vale, Hunter Valley).

Aromas: Bramble jelly, blueberry, black cherry, white pepper, violet.

Main wine styles: Syrah is another of the deeply pigmented black grapes, so most examples have a saturated purple colour when young. A ripe dark fruit character is almost invariably present on the nose. Really great Syrah, in both Australia and France, will have an extra dimension of floral and pepper notes. With bottle age dried fruit aromas come to dominate the nose, along with earthy, savoury, leathery notes.

Syrah wines tend to be quite big in the mouth. Although wines made from Syrah often carry a decent thwack of tannin, you are rarely conscious of this because of the lushness of the fruit and the lowish acidity.

GRENACHE (GARNACHA)

Home patch: Spain, France (Rhône).

Successes elsewhere: Australia.

Aromas: Jammy red fruits, spicy, herbal.

Main wine styles: 'Up front' just about sums up the Grenache. The wines made from Grenache are never particularly deeply coloured. You can get a fantastic attack of over-ripe red fruits on the nose, followed by some spicy notes. Broad and soft in the mouth, acidity and tannin levels are usually relatively low. The knock-out blow on Grenache comes from the alcohol, which is often 14%ABV or more. Grenache is also used to make some delicious rosés.

GAMAY

Home patch: France (Burgundy).

Successes elsewhere: Mercifully none.

Aromas: Tinned strawberries, other soft red fruits, banana.

Main wine styles: Friendly, fruity, quaffing wines, with soft tannins and low acidity. A few of the top Cru Beaujolais (most famously Moulin-à-Vent) have a bit more density and structure, but these are the exceptions rather than the rule.

MOURVEDRE (MATARO, MONASTRELL)

Home patch: Spain, France (Rhône, Provence).

Successes elsewhere: Australia, California.

Aromas: Dark fruits, black pepper.

Main wine styles: Although rarely used on its own, Mourvèdre is an important part of the southern Rhône blend. It produces deeply coloured wines that are not particularly aromatic (hence the advantage of blending in some Syrah and/or Grenache). On the palate Mourvèdre can be fearsomely astringent and tannic (one of its nicknames is 'dog-strangler').

TEMPRANILLO (TINTA RORIZ)

Home patch: Spain (Rioja, Navarra, Ribera del Duero).

Successes elsewhere: Portugal, Argentina.

Aromas: Berry fruits, spices.

Main wine styles: Youthful, inexpensive Tempranillo wines have a fairly deep colour, some soft red and black fruit aromas, and a rounded mid-bodied palate. There may or may not be a whiff of American oak on the nose. With extended wood ageing a very different beast emerges. An old-fashioned Gran Reserva Rioja is a faded terracotta colour, with a creamy and figgy bouquet. The palate will be smooth and harmonious.

SANGIOVESE

Home patch: Italy (Tuscany).

Successes elsewhere: California.

Aromas: Bitter cherry, raspberry, almond.

Main wine styles: Sangiovese produces moderately coloured red wines. There is always something slightly austere and astringent about the red fruit character of Sangiovese. The wines are generally mid-bodied on the palate, with a twang of acid and cherry stone tannin.

NEBBIOLO (SPANNA)

Home patch: Italy (Piemonte).

Successes elsewhere: Very few. One or two laudable efforts in California.

Aromas: Damson, prune, liquorice, tar.

Main wine styles: The colour of a top Nebbiolo can often be deceptively pale, fading to tawny quite early in its life. What bowls over Nebbiolo fans is the complex aroma, different from any other black grape variety. Although not particularly rich, with its astringent tannins, high acidity and warm alcohol, Nebbiolo can take some wrestling to the ground.

Top: Pinot Noir.
Centre: Gamay.
Bottom: Mourvèdre.

47

Grape varieties

ZINFANDEL (PRIMITIVO)

Home patch: California, Italy (Puglia).

Successes elsewhere: n/a.

Aromas: Super ripe red fruits (particularly strawberry), spicy.

Main wine styles: The ampelographers (vine experts) blow hot and cold as to whether California's Zinfandel is the same as Puglia's Primitivo. A big-hitting red Zinfandel has a deepish colour, followed by lush, juicy, spicy red fruit. The palate is warm and enticing, with plenty of fruit and softish acidity. Scary alcohol levels can be achieved (over 15%ABV sometimes). Zinfandel is also used to produce medium rosés, which are marketed as 'White Zinfandel' or 'Blush'.

PINOTAGE

Home patch: South Africa.

Successes elsewhere: n/a.

Aromas: Berry jam, smoke, coal dust.

Main wine styles: Most Pinotages are mid-bodied, although one or two chunkier examples are made. The tannin and acidity levels are quite low. There is plenty of soft, jammy fruit on the nose. The Pinotage tends to produce wines with a moderate depth of colour.

CLONES

Getting to grips with the world's main grape varieties is a hard enough task for most wine lovers. For grape growers, there is a further level of complexity concerning the different 'clones' of each variety. Ampelographers have realised that there are distinct 'versions' of grape varieties like Pinot Noir. These different strains are referred to as clones. Clone A might carry a heavier crop than clone B, but clone B might produce the superior wine. Growers have to balance the merits of the different clones before deciding what to plant. The emphasis used to be on planting the 'best' clone of any variety. Now, many growers plant a number of clones with the aim of obtaining more complexity.

VARIETAL LABELLING

Many wines now display on their labels the names of the grape varieties they were made from. Such a wine is referred to as a 'varietal'. Where a wine is named after its region of origin, rather than its variety, the term 'generic' is used.

The EU rules for labelling specify that if a single grape name is shown (e.g. Chardonnay), then that variety has to account for at least 85% of what is in the bottle. If two varieties are shown (e.g. Marsanne-Chardonnay), then these two varieties have to make up 100% of the blend. The first named grape has to account for the majority of the mix. Up to five varieties can now be shown on a label, in descending order of contribution.

More about grape varieties

Most of the famous grape varieties have been with us for centuries. For instance, one theory has it that what we now call Riesling was growing wild in Germany 2000 years ago. However, as with most crops grown today, growers have tried to develop 'new' vines that improve on the existing varieties. Three techniques have been used to create new grape varieties.

Crossing

This involves cross-pollinating two varieties of *Vitis vinifera*. The seeds from the cross are planted and the offspring screened for required traits. Pinotage was developed in South Africa by crossing Pinot Noir and Cinsaut. The logic was to get a vine that had the quality of Pinot Noir, but like Cinsaut, was adapted to a hot climate. The other famous cross is Müller-Thurgau. One parent may have been Riesling, but nobody is sure what it was crossed with – possibly Silvaner, Chasselas or another Riesling.

Interspecific crossing (producing a hybrid vine)

In this version of crossing, one parent is *Vitis vinifera* and the other is an American vine. The logic here is to capture the quality of a European vine whilst introducing the resilience of the American vine. The development of hybrid vines was one of the initial responses to the *Phylloxera* epidemic in the nineteenth century *(see page 39)*. Unfortunately the quality of wine produced by many of these early hybrids was not impressive. With the general adoption of grafting, the growing of hybrid vines came to be disparaged. In the European Union hybrid vines can be used only in Table Wine production. However, there are still cool climate grape growing countries, like England and Canada, where the sheer toughness of hybrid vines outweighs the perceived disadvantages. Seyval Blanc is probably the most famous of the hybrid vines.

Clonal selection

This technique can be used where different clones *(see above)* of a grape variety exist. When a vineyard comes to be re-planted, the grower has to decide which old vine to take the cuttings from. If over a period of several vine generations cuttings are always taken from vines showing a particular trait (e.g. early ripening or intensely flavoured grapes), then eventually a 'super' vine will emerge. The most famous example of a vine developed by clonal selection was Gewürztraminer. The original Traminer vine (which is still grown) has a relatively delicate perfume. It was by always selecting from the vine that produced the most aromatic grapes that the intensely scented Gewürztraminer came about.

Winemaking

Although there are many fancy tweaks used in winemaking nowadays, the fundamental process of fermenting wine has not changed that much in millennia. I have described white winemaking in some detail, then concentrated on what makes the production of red and rosé wine different.

In some cases the individual (or estate) who grew the grapes will also make the wine. However, the capital cost of owning a winery is prohibitive for many grape growers. What is more, some may lack the expertise or motivation to make their own wine. In these circumstances two options exist. The grower can sell his grapes to a commercial winery, which will subsequently make the wine and market it. The other option is for the grower to be a member of a co-operative winery. He will deliver his grapes to the jointly owned winery, which will produce the wine and sell it. The grower will then be paid a dividend based on the tonnage of grapes he delivered.

MAKING WHITE WINE

Although most white wines are made from white grapes, with some care it is also possible to make a white wine from black grapes (Champagne is the best example of a white wine made primarily from black grapes). This is possible because white wine is produced by fermenting only the juice of the grape.

Crushing and pressing

In white wine production the grapes will normally be crushed and de-stalked before being pumped to the presses. By gently pressing the grapes the juice (also known as 'must') will be released. Some winemakers delay the pressing for a few hours, allowing the grape skins to soak in the juice. This process is referred to as 'skin contact', and it increases the flavour extraction from the skins. By contrast, some winemakers seek to avoid any skin contact and therefore put uncrushed (and un-de-stalked!) grapes directly into the press. This process is referred to as 'whole cluster pressing'.

Presses come in various shapes and sizes. The old-fashioned vertical (or basket) press is still used in some places for relatively small batches of grapes. However, large horizontal presses have taken over in most wineries. These work either by metal plates moving in from either end of the press squeezing the grapes in the middle, or by a rubber bag being inflated inside the press. Either way, grape juice will run out through the slatted sides of the press. Most of the must will be released during a first gentle pressing. Once this is completed the mass of skins, pulp and pips can be broken up and pressed for a second time. More force is applied during the second pressing, and the resulting juice is of a lower grade than that obtained from the first pressing. Some wineries will ferment this 'second pressing' must separately from the 'first pressing' must, and decide whether to blend the two only during the maturation period. The pressing cycle can be repeated one more time to obtain some 'third pressing' must, but the volumes are small. However, the ingenuity of the wine producer is not exhausted. In some parts of Europe the dry skins and pips from the presses will be soaked in water, fermented and distilled. The resulting spirit is called 'grappa' in Italy and 'eau-de-vie de marc' in France.

Boosting sugar content of the must

Grape juice running from the press is quite cloudy so it is usually allowed to settle for a few hours. During this time the winemaker can check the composition of the grape must. The most critical variable is the sugar content of the juice. In a perfect world the must would have just the right amount of natural sugar to provide the required amount of alcohol when the fermentation is completed. However, in cool climate regions it is not uncommon for the must to be slightly deficient in sugar. All is not lost, as winemakers in these regions are allowed to add beet or cane sugar to the must to boost its sugar content. This process is referred to as 'chaptalisation'. Bear in mind this sugar will be converted into alcohol, so chaptalisation is not a way of sweetening wine but rather a way to raise its level of alcohol.

Ripe, healthy Chardonnay grapes arriving at the Stag's Leap Winery in the Napa Valley, California.

Hi-tech – temperature-controlled stainless steel vats in the open air right next to the vineyard that produces the fruit.

contain plenty of sugar, but they often lack acidity. Hence winemakers in hot climate regions often have to 'acidify' their musts. This is achieved by adding tartaric acid (tartaric acid is after all the main acid in grapes).

Preserving the must

The other compound that is almost invariably added to the must is sulphur dioxide (SO_2). Even in small doses sulphur dioxide has three important properties that are of use to the winemaker:

Sulphur dioxide kills wild yeast These yeast are found growing on the skins of grapes as part of the bloom. It would have been wild yeast that fermented the wines drunk in ancient times. However, there are many different strains of wild yeast, some of which can produce off flavours in the wine. What is more, most wild yeast die when the alcohol level is around only 4%ABV. By knocking out the wild yeast the way is cleared for a wine yeast to ferment the must.

Sulphur dioxide kills bacteria *Acetobacter* can attack grape juice or wine and turn it into vinegar (*see page 26*). Good cellar hygiene and the use of sulphur dioxide are the main reasons why wine vinegar is something we put on our salads nowadays rather than drink.

Sulphur dioxide is an anti-oxidant Too much air contact at any stage of a wine's life can cause oxidation (*see page 26*). As well as avoiding exposure to the air, the judicious use of sulphur dioxide can mop up oxygen present in the wine. Many winemakers will ensure that there is some active sulphur dioxide present in their wines right through the production process.

It is, however, worth saying that the use of additives outlined above is strictly controlled. What is more, many of these practices have been with us for a long time.

Modifying the acidity of the must

When there has been a very cool summer, as well as lacking in sugar, the must may be excessively acidic. The winemaker can correct this imbalance by 'de-acidifying'. This is usually achieved by adding potassium bicarbonate to the must. Chaptalisation and de-acidification are techniques that have to be employed in cool climate regions. Growing grapes in hot climates though is not without its problems. At harvest the grapes usually

Fermenting the must

After any heavy particles have settled out of the must, the juice can be drained off the sediment (running must or wine off a sediment is called 'racking'). The clarified must can then be fermented. Fermentation is the biochemical reaction that makes life tolerable on this planet. Yeast will attack the sugar and convert it into ethanol (ethyl alcohol) and carbon dioxide. Heat is liberated by the transformation. Non-chemists may look away at this stage:

$$C_6H_{12}O_6 => 2C_2H_5OH + 2CO_2 + Heat$$

sugar   ethanol   carbon dioxide

Selecting the yeast

Having killed the wild yeast, most winemakers will introduce a pre-selected strain of cultured wine yeast to carry out the fermentation. Cultured yeast can ferment right up to 15%ABV and will impart clean aromas to the wine. The more traditional approach used in places like Burgundy is to allow a natural wine yeast to ferment the wine. Having killed the wild yeast by adding sulphur dioxide, strains of natural wine yeast present in the winery are allowed to initiate the fermentation. This is a slower and slightly more risky process, but the Burgundians would say that the natural yeast are part of the uniqueness of their region, and give a wine more complexity than could be achieved by using a cultured yeast.

Critical temperatures

Wine yeast can function at temperatures as low as 4°C (40°F) and as high as 35°C (95°F). Obviously the higher the temperature the quicker the fermentation. White wines are fermented at quite low temperatures, usually between 15°C (59°F) and 20°C (68°F), to maintain their attractive freshness. Given that the fermentation reaction produces heat, it is normally necessary to cool the wine as it is fermenting. A fermentation at 15–20°C (59–68°F) will take about two weeks to complete.

Steel, concrete or cask?

Nowadays most white wines are fermented in stainless steel vats. Stainless steel is easy to clean and can be sterilised. What is more, being a good conductor of heat, it is relatively easy to cool a stainless steel vat during the fermentation. Some vats are built with integral cooling coils or jackets, but the simplest way to cool a stainless steel vat is to run cold water down the outside. Modern wineries have this whole cooling regime computer controlled, with each vat capable of being pre-programmed to ferment at a particular temperature. Concrete vats (lined with tiles or resin) and large old wooden vats are rarely used today as they are hard to clean and temperature control is more difficult (concrete and wood are good insulators). What are used for fermenting some of the world's top dry white wines, particularly Chardonnays, are small new oak barrels. Fermenting and maturing in cask allows a

Lo-tech – topping up the oak barrels by hand (however, have you ever seen such a clean watering can?).

The raw material starts its journey from vineyard to winery.

milk. Hence a wine that undergoes malolactic fermentation will end up with a softer, less acid palate than one where the transformation has been blocked. Malolactic fermentation affects the nose of a wine as well, giving it a broader, more buttery type of aroma.

There are no hard and fast rules saying specific white wines must or must not undergo malolactic fermentation. However, the softening of the acidity and the butteriness on the nose add to the character and complexity of most Chardonnays. By contrast, the fresh acidity and vibrant green fruit aromas of Sauvignon Blanc wines would be spoilt by malolactic fermentation. To encourage malolactic fermentation, wines are left on the lees and the vat is kept warm after the end of the alcoholic fermentation. If the native bacteria are reluctant to start the transformation a culture can be added. To block the malolactic fermentation the vat is chilled, some sulphur dioxide is added and the wine is racked off its lees.

more gentle pick-up of oak flavour than is achieved by fermenting in stainless steel and then putting the wine into wood. With these barrels being new and small, the problems of cleanliness and temperature control are not significant.

Malolactic fermentation

At the end of the fermentation all the sugar will have been converted into alcohol and carbon dioxide, leaving a dry white wine. The yeast gradually sink to the bottom of the vat, forming a sediment called 'lees'. It is at this stage that wine can undergo a second transformation, known as malolactic fermentation. In malolactic fermentation the malic acid in the wine is converted into lactic acid and carbon dioxide. Naturally occurring bacteria in the lees are responsible for malolactic fermentation. Malic acid originates in the grapes and has a sharp, sour, green taste. Lactic acid is the acid found in dairy products like butter and

Racking and maturing the wine

Whether or not the wine has undergone malolactic fermentation it will eventually be racked off its lees. The wine can then be matured. Most white wines undergo only a short period of maturation, somewhere in the region of six months. This is because white wines are delicate in nature and long maturation would dry out their fruit. The maturation of most white wines takes place in stainless steel or concrete vats, which of course impart no flavour to the wine. However, a few premium white wines, particularly Chardonnays, will be matured in oak barrels, often the same ones that they fermented in (*see above*). If this is the case, the maturation takes place without racking. In other words, the wine matures on its yeast lees. This contributes to the richness and complexity of many top Chardonnays, particularly the great white Burgundies. In fact, some winemakers actually stir up the lees to release even more flavour (a process called 'bâtonnage').

Barrels, barriques – and chips

Once upon a time wooden barrels were merely used as a way of transporting wine. Scant attention would have been paid to the type of oak, the barrel's age, or the cooper who made it, as long as the damned thing did not leak. Today, the science and technology of barrels is an important part of oenology (the study of wine). That said, all the barrels used in winemaking are still hand-made (a great craft well worth seeing first hand). In the past, barrels were made from various types of wood, but the consensus these days is that oak is best. It is only oak that has the lovely spicy, toasty, vanilla character beloved of many wine drinkers. If a white wine is going to be aged in barrels then it is usually French oak that is used.

For a barrel to impart the maximum oak flavour to a wine it will have to be small and brand new. The normal size of the small oak barrels used in most cellars is called a 'barrique' and has a capacity of 225 litres (59 US gallons). The larger the barrel, the less oak flavour will get into the wine. What is more, each time a barrel is used there will be a decreasing amount of oakiness that can be extracted. After it has been used three times most of the oak flavour will have been extracted from the wood (although as a storage vessel it would be good for decades longer). Another factor that has bearing on oak maturation is the cost of the barrels. A new French oak barrique costs about £350, yet will be capable of holding only 300 bottles of wine. So when you consider the cost of a fancy Chardonnay that has

More about filters

There are three main types of filter used for wine.

Kieselguhr, or diatomaceous earth

This is the coarsest grade of filter and involves pumping the wine through what to the layman looks like mud. It is useful as a first stage in cleaning up a very cloudy wine containing a lot of yeast and other suspended matter.

Cellulose

Cellulose filter pads look like giant, square coffee filters. When a wine is pumped through a cellulose filter pad, yeast and bacteria are absorbed by the cellulose fibres. The filter pads are arranged in a steel 'plate and frame' structure.

Membrane

Nylon filter pads are now available with pores so fine that all remaining yeast and bacteria can be removed from the wine. The winemaker can be sure that what goes into bottle is sterile. This allows most wine to be bottled cold. In the past, the only way to be sure that all the microbes in a wine were dead was to pasteurise the wine. However, heating the wine in this way inevitably compromised its quality.

been aged in new oak barrels, remember that over a £1 per bottle went into buying the wood.

Given the cost of oak barrels, it is not surprising that winemakers have come up with other ways of getting oak flavour into a wine. The commonest technique is to dunk a bag of oak chips into a vat of wine for a few weeks. This trick will give the wine some instant oak flavour but of course will not impart the elegant toastiness that comes from barrel ageing.

Because of evaporation and wine soaking into the wood, every few days the barrels have to be topped up with wine from the same batch. A bung is kept in the top to keep out air and insects. The maturation period gives the winemaker a chance to compose the final blend (whether to use first and second pressings, or whether to combine two or more grape varieties etc.).

Which wine would you choose? A white wine before and after filtration through Kieselguhr.

Cleaning up the wine

Once the wine has been matured it needs to be cleaned up and prepared for bottling. Several processes are used to clarify and stabilise the wine:

Fining Even after six months of ageing in barrel or vat a white wine can still be slightly hazy. Fining is the technique used to remove haze from a wine. In the case of white wine, a fining agent called bentonite (a special type of clay) is poured into the top of the barrel or vat. Over a period of about a week the fining agent sinks down through the wine, picking up the haze material as it goes. Once the fining agent has formed a sediment at the bottom of the vessel the clarified white wine can be racked off.

Centrifugation If a wine contains a lot of suspended yeast these can be removed by centrifugation. The wine is spun at high speed, the centrifugal force throwing the yeast out. One of the great advantages of a centrifuge is that it can be used to treat thousands of litres of wine at a time.

Cold treatment Winemakers use cold treatment as a way of minimising the risk of a wine subsequently forming tartrate crystals in the bottle (*see page 27*). A week or so before the wine is to be bottled it is placed in an insulated vat and chilled down to -3°C (27°F). By holding the wine at this temperature for a week, any excess salts of tartaric acid will crystallise in the vat. Once drained out of the vat, the chances of the wine subsequently forming tartrate crystals are less.

Filtration Filtration is used just before bottling to make sure that there are no remaining yeast or bacteria in the wine (*see chart on page 55*).

Although all of these cleaning up processes have their uses, there is a danger that if used indiscriminately the winemaker ends up with a wine that is clear and stable, but has been stripped of all body and personality. The skill is to do just enough to the wine to ensure that it reaches the customer in good condition, whilst minimising any loss of character. For instance, several top white Burgundy producers gently fine their white wines with bentonite and filter only once through cellulose.

Bottling the wine

Bottling halls are hardly the most thrilling places on earth. Most bottling is now done under hygienic conditions to minimise the risk of yeast contamination. Various systems are also employed to keep any air contact to a minimum.

Sealing the bottle

The one big worry many wine producers have at the bottling stage is not the bottle but the cork. The high price of natural cork, combined with the incidence of cork taint (*see page 26*), has led wineries to search for alternative closures. Synthetic (plastic) corks are seen quite widely these days. They seem to be a perfectly effective way of making sure that a wine for early drinking reaches the final consumer in good nick. You still need to go through the rigmarole of opening the bottle with a corkscrew, a ritual that is part of the 'wine experience' for many drinkers. What we do not know at the moment is how synthetic corks perform over 20 or 30 years in the neck of a bottle. This, and the whole image of a plastic closure, means that nearly all fine wines are still closed with a natural cork.

Screw tops are another efficient and dependable way of sealing wine bottles. Even more than plastic corks though, the image of wine in a screw-top bottle is not good. The problem goes back to the days when some of the first wine in screw-top bottles was plonk. Hence the consumer came to associate screw-top bottles with rot gut wine. It is odd that we are quite happy to have premium spirits in screw-top bottles, but shirk away from wine in the same packaging format.

The alternative wine dispense system that has caught on in markets like Australia and the UK is bag-in-box. Many consumers are happy with the convenience provided by a 3 litre (6 US pint) box in the fridge or the kitchen. The technology of the format has been improved over the years to ensure that the wine stays fresh before and after the pack has been opened.

MAKING RED WINE

Whilst you can get away with using white and black grapes to make a white wine, with red wine you have to use black grapes. The black grapes are crushed and de-stalked before being pumped straight to the fermentation vat. A few winemakers will allow some stalks into the fermentation vat, but the stalks have to be very ripe if the wine is not to pick up harsh green tannins. Any adjustments that need to be made to the must, such as the addition of sulphur dioxide, chaptalisation and the introduction of cultured yeast, are all made direct to the fermentation vat.

Skin contact

The essence of red wine production is that the wine will ferment in contact with the black grape skins. As the fermentation proceeds the wine extracts colour, tannin and flavour from the skins. Most of the colour tends to be extracted at the beginning of the fermentation, whereas the tannin is released as the alcohol level rises. The extraction is aided by heat. For this reason most red wines ferment at 25–30°C (77–85°F). At this temperature it takes the yeast about a week to convert all the sugar into alcohol and carbon dioxide.

Mixing in the cap One slightly awkward aspect of fermenting red wine is that bubbles of carbon dioxide stick to the grape skins, causing them to float to the surface of the wine. This thick layer of skins is referred to as the 'cap'. To make sure that the cap is mixed with the fermenting wine various techniques are used. 'Pumping over' (*remontage* in French) involves draining fermenting wine out of the bottom of the vat, pumping it up to the top of

'The frisson created by the sight of the bottling line tested Jemima's restraint to the limit.'

the vat and then spraying it over the cap. The slight aeration that the wine receives at this stage is actually no bad thing, as a little oxygen helps yeast growth. 'Punching down' (*pigeage* in French) involves pushing the skins down into the fermenting wine with a device that looks like an oar. Some fermentation vats, called 'rotary fermenters', have been specially rigged up to rotate on their axes, mixing the skins and wine as they turn. Just a few wines, most famously in Portugal, are still trodden to ensure that the skins and wine are well mixed.

Running the wine off the skins Given that extraction is taking place all the time that the skins and wine are together, one of the crucial decisions when making red wine is at what stage should the wine be run off the skins. If the skins and wine are separated after just a few days, the resulting red wine may have a deep colour but it will be relatively light in tannin. By contrast, if the skins are left to soak in the wine for several weeks after the fermentation has finished (a process called 'cuvaison'), an intensely tannic wine will result. By the way, this is part of the reason why classic young Clarets are so tannic.

Free run and press wine

When the decision is taken to drain a vat, about 90% of the wine will run out under gravity. This fraction is known as the 'free run wine'. The skins and pips that are left in the vat are then shovelled into a press. The remaining 10% of the liquid is squeezed out of the skins. The resulting 'press wine' is deeply coloured and profoundly tannic. The free run wine and the press wine will be matured separately, with a decision about blending being taken during maturation. A good slug of press wine in the final blend will help to give a wine the sort of structure it needs for long maturation. By contrast, if a supple early drinking red wine is required, little or no press wine may be used in the final blend.

Malolactic fermentation

The newly fermented red wine will be allowed to rest in the vat for a few weeks, during which time the lees form. It is at this stage that a red wine undergoes malolactic fermentation (*see page 54*). Unlike white wine where the decision whether to encourage or block malolactic fermentation is a question of style, with red wine the process is always encouraged (if necessary by warming the cellar). The reason is to do with balancing the structure of a red wine. Reds have a tannic astringency on the palate that would be exagger-

Punching down the cap (and not the insertion of an endoscope into the author's liver!).

Making wine

ated by the presence of malic acid. Lactic acid, being softer, makes the tannins taste less harsh. This softening effect of malolactic fermentation is even more pronounced if the transformation takes place in barrel. Hence the current fashion for malolactic fermentation in barrel when the wines are going to be sold 'en primeur' (*see page 72*).

Maturing red wine

With malolactic fermentation completed the wine will be racked and maturation can start. It is probably fair to say that most top-quality red wines will see some oak maturation. Red wines, being more robust than white wines, generally receive a longer maturation in barrel. The average these days is probably about 18 months to two years, although one or two reds do get much longer than this. The same size of barrique, 225 litres (59 US gallons), is used as for the white wines. The red winemaker has an extra option when it comes to the type of oak used to make the barrels. Many red wines are matured in the same sort of French oak barrels that are used for white wines. This oak contributes a subtle, spicy toastiness to the wine. Most of the world's Pinot Noirs will benefit from this type of wood. If the barrels are made out of American oak by contrast, the wine will pick up a heavier, creamier, vanilla character. This robust oakiness is part of the flavour of most Riojas and a lot of Australia's finest Shiraz. As well as being topped up regularly, red wines maturing in the barrel have to be racked every three months or so. This is to remove the sediment that forms in the barrels as the tannin and colouring matter in the wine start to fall out. Leaving a red wine resting on this sediment can sometimes taint its flavour.

Not all red wines will be aged in barrel. Given the cost of barriques nowadays most cheap and cheerful wines see no oak at all (except maybe the odd chip). Some fruity vibrant red wines, like Beaujolais, would actually be spoilt if matured in new oak.

Preparing for bottling

With the maturation completed and the final blend put together, the wine just needs to be prepared for bottling. The same clarifying and stabilising options exist as for white wine: fining, centrifugation, cold treatment and filtration. The main fining agent for red wine is egg white rather than bentonite. Traditionally the beaten whites of six eggs are added to each barrique. As well as clarifying the red wine, the egg white (being a protein) will remove some of the bitter tannins from the wine. For premium red wines the fashion is to do as little as possible to the wine before bottling. A lot of these wines will be bottled without fining or filtration. This increases the chances of the wine throwing a sediment, but less character will have been stripped from the wine unnecessarily.

Alternative treatments

The classic process for producing a red wine outlined above is all well and good for premium wines that will benefit from some maturation. The weakness is that in most circumstances the producer has to wait for two years or more before the wine reaches the market. A couple of techniques have been developed to produce a red wine that is ready to drink within months rather than years of the harvest.

Carbonic maceration Carbonic maceration (*macération carbonique* in French) involves taking whole bunches of black grapes and sealing them in a vat. The atmosphere of carbon dioxide that forms in the vat (or is injected) causes the colour in the grape skins to leak into the pulp. When the vat is emptied and the grapes pressed, red juice

Drying grapes indoors to make Recioto della Valpolicella.

mented. This process does alter the varietal character of the grapes used and, whilst the wines are deeply coloured when young, there has always been a question mark over the long-term stability of the colour.

MAKING ROSE WINE

The vast majority of rosé wines are not made by the obvious route of adding a dash of red wine to a vat of white wine (although pink Champagne is usually made this way). Most rosés are made by de-stalking and crushing black grapes, and then leaving the skins soaking in the juice for a few hours. In this time a small amount of pink colour is extracted from the skins. Just exactly how long the skins and juice stay together depends on the grape variety being used and the depth of pinkness required. Once the pink juice has been drained off the skins the fermentation will be handled just like a white wine.

Rosés are matured for only a short time before bottling. It is worth being aware that rosé wines (again with the exception of Champagne) do not age particularly well. You should always buy the youngest vintage available.

MAKING SWEET WINE

The one way you are never normally allowed to make a wine sweet is by just dumping in sugar. Chaptalisation, the process of adding sugar to grape must, is permitted in many countries, but all of this sugar will be converted into alcohol during the fermentation. Adding sugar to a finished wine is illegal in most cases.

Sweetness in wine is achieved by using one of the following techniques:

Using grapes with a huge amount of sugar

If yeast try to ferment very sweet grape must, the whole process will proceed slowly. Assuming the

runs out. Crucially the tannins stay behind in the skins. The red juice is fermented and produces a wine that has a deep red colour, plenty of immediate jammy fruit, but very little tannin. Such a wine is ready to drink immediately. The Achilles' heel of wines made this way is that because they contain less tannin than a normal red wine they do not keep well. Beaujolais Nouveau is the most famous wine made by carbonic maceration. Many other Beaujolais wines are made by *semi-macération carbonique* where whole bunches are fermented in an open vat.

Thermovinification This involves rapidly heating crushed black grapes before the fermentation. A large amount of colour is released in a matter of minutes. The must is then cooled down and fer-

yeast can keep going, there comes a point when the alcohol gets up to around 14–15%ABV that the yeast start to die. This brings the fermentation to a natural halt, leaving any residual sugar to give the wine its sweetness. There are several ways of achieving heroic grape sugar levels, as indicated in the chart, right. Although these processes produce the world's great sweet wines, they are all highly labour intensive, very often risky, and are generally carried out on a small scale. In other words, these wines are going to be expensive.

Adding grape must (*süssreserve*)

This technique involves setting aside a small amount of grape must at harvest time and preventing it from fermenting. The rest of the must will be fermented and a dry white wine produced. Just before bottling, the dry white wine and the grape must are blended. The medium sweetness of many inexpensive German wines such as Liebfraumilch and Piesporter Michelsberg is achieved by the addition of *süssreserve*.

Adding RCM

An even cheaper sweetening agent than normal grape must is rectified concentrated must (RCM). By evaporating off most of its water content and purifying it further, grape must can be turned into RCM. This neutral syrup is used to sweeten basic wines like French Vin de Table.

Stopping the fermentation

If a normal fermentation is arrested part way through, a sweet wine will result. The earlier the fermentation process is stopped, the sweeter the wine will be. At the same time, the earlier the fermentation is stopped, the less alcoholic the wine will be. The sweetness in White Zinfandel and Asti comes from an arrested fermentation.

Fermentation can be stopped or prevented by using one or more of the following techniques: refrigeration below 4°C (40°F); filtration; racking;

Achieving high sugar levels

Over the centuries, probably more time, ingenuity and effort have gone into crafting sweet wines than any other style of wine.

Noble Rot

The mould *Botrytis cinerea (see page 40)* causes the grapes to shrivel up, so concentrating the sugars. The concentrating effect of the Noble Rot is not just confined to the sugars. Because most of the grape's other components are concentrated at the same time you get a wine with incredible weight and power. This is the reason why the world's great Noble Rot wines are so long lived. The most famous example is Sauternes.

Frozen grapes

In this case grapes are left on the vine until the winter. The growers wait until the first severe frost occurs, -8°C (18°F), before sending the pickers out into the vineyard. The frozen grapes are returned to the winery as quickly as possible and then gently pressed. Most of the water stays frozen inside the grape, so the juice that oozes out is very sweet. This technique is used in Germany, Austria and also Canada to produce Eiswein / Ice Wine.

Grapes dried out of doors

In hot climates it is possible to pick grapes and then lay them on straw mats, in the sun, to dry out. These raisins will tend to give a heavy, dark sweet wine. The Pedro Ximenez sweetening wine used in Sherry production is made this way.

Grapes dried on the vine

In areas that have fine autumn weather, grapes will sometimes desiccate on the vine without the intervention of Noble Rot. Probably the most famous example of this in France is Jurançon.

Grapes dried indoors

A more dependable (not at the mercy of the elements) and gentler way to dry the grapes is to bring them indoors. The bunches are laid on racks or mats and left to dry for anything from a week to several months. Italy's passito (made from dried grapes) wines such as Recioto della Valpolicella and Vin Santo are made this way, as are Vin de Paille (in the Jura region of France) and Strohwein (Austria).

centrifugation; addition of sulphur dioxide; pressure; addition of brandy (this is how fortified wines like Port are produced).

MAKING SPARKLING WINE

There are a number of ways of making sparkling wines. The main techniques are as follows:

Traditional method

The details of this method (formerly called *Méthode Champenoise*) as practised in Champagne are described on page 86. The principle is to take a dry base wine, then by adding sugar and yeast stimulate a second fermentation in the bottle. Once the wine is sparkling the yeast are removed by *remuage* and *dégorgement*. As well as Champagne, most of France's other Appellation Contrôlée sparkling wines are made this way, for example Saumur and Blanquette de Limoux. Cava, Spain's quality sparkling wine, is also made by the traditional method, as are the best of the New World's sparkling wines.

Transfer method

Like the traditional method, the transfer method involves a second fermentation in the bottle to obtain the sparkle. However, instead of the expense of *remuage* and *dégorgement*, in the transfer method the bottles, yeast and all, are emptied out. The yeast is then removed from the wine by filtration. The wine is returned to a fresh bottle. The whole process is carried out in a closed system to prevent any loss of pressure. This transfer method is used at some wineries in the New World.

Tank method

Sometimes called *cuve close* or 'Charmat' method, the tank method involves stimulating a second fermentation in a large closed tank, rather than in a bottle. Once the wine is sparkling it is drained completely from the tank, filtered to remove all the yeast and then bottled. Thousands of litres of wine can be produced in one batch, making it much cheaper than bottle fermentation. That said, many tank method sparkling wines have a raw greenness on the palate and a somewhat confected aroma. Most Sekt (the German sparkling wine) and cheap French Vin Mousseux are made this way.

Asti method

Asti is made by a variation on the tank method. Rather than getting its sparkle from a second fermentation in the tank, the fizz in Asti comes from a first fermentation in the tank. What is more, by arresting the fermentation half-way through, it ends up being medium sweet and also low in alcohol (7.5%ABV).

Injection method

This method (also known as 'carbonation' or the 'bicycle pump' method) is the cheapest way of making sparkling wine. Carbon dioxide is injected into refrigerated wine and er... that's it. Rather like other carbonated drinks, the bubbles dissipate quickly. By contrast, sparkling wines made by the tank method, and particularly those made by the traditional method, can maintain streamers of small bubbles in the glass for half an hour or more. What is more, the traditional method actually generates a lot of the complex flavours in Champagne.

MAKING FORTIFIED WINE

Under normal circumstances yeast cannot ferment much above 15%ABV. If a wine is required with a strength higher than this, grape spirit (water white, newly distilled brandy, often at 96%ABV) must be added. In the case of Sherry, the spirit is added once the fermentation has finished. By contrast, in the making of Port the spirit is added during the fermentation process. Madeira can in fact be made in both ways. The details of the production of Sherry, Port, Madeira and the other main fortified wines are described in 'The World of Wine' section (*see page 64*).

MAKING WINES WITH LESS ALCOHOL THAN NORMAL

A number of grape-based products exist with less than 5.5%ABV. There are three main production techniques. The fermentation can be stopped using exactly the same processes employed in making some of the sweeter wines, except that in this case they are applied earlier in the fermentation. The alcohol can be removed using various methods including vacuum distillation and reverse osmosis. Thirdly, the wine can actually be diluted by adding mineral water or fruit juice; such products are sometimes referred to as 'coolers'. There is no getting around the fact that the production processes, and the absence of the flavour and texture of the alcohol, result in products that are fundamentally different from 'real' wine.

Fact Box

Legal descriptions

In the UK the labelling of these products is prone to cause confusion; bear in mind that the following descriptions strictly delineate the alcohol content.

Non-alcoholic
0%ABV.

Alcohol free
less than 0.05%ABV.

Dealcoholised
less than 0.5%ABV.

Low alcohol
0.5–1.2%ABV.

Reduced alcohol
1.2–5.5%ABV.

Treading the grapes to make Port (don't even think about it!).

The world
of wine

Although great wines are now being made in many parts of the world, France still produces the biggest range of fine wines. There will always be a demand for the profound wines of Bordeaux, Burgundy and the Rhône despite the high prices. The best of these wines combine concentration and elegance, structure and harmony.

At the other end of the scale, there will always be a huge demand for decent quaffing wines. One French region that has very successfully re-invented itself as a

France

major supplier of well-made, inexpensive varietal wines is Languedoc-Roussillon.

If France has a weakness then it is with its mass of rather amorphous mid-market wines. Wines such as Entre-Deux-Mers, Muscadet, Beaujolais, Côtes du Rhône and Corbières are all right, but they are rarely anything to write home about. These wines often seem austere and lean to someone whose palate has grown used to the vibrant, unsubtle flavours of most of the New World wines.

A good communication and marketing job has to be done as well. The new generation of wine drinkers in places like the UK is the first one to grow up without being raised on the 'France makes the greatest wine' message. A youngster's experience of wine may well have been formed on the vast array of New World varietal wines. Why should they try Sancerre, when their whole experience of Sauvignon Blanc has been through drinking bottles of Chilean and New Zealand wine?

The world of wine

French wine law

In terms of volume, France is the world's second largest wine producer (Italy produces just a tad more). It is worth understanding how the French categorise their wines, as the classification system used in France has been the blueprint for the wine laws of the other European Union (EU) countries.

All the wines produced in the EU are classified as either 'Table Wines' or 'Quality Wines Produced in a Specified Region' (QWPSR). Generally speaking, Table Wines are simple, inexpensive wines, with fairly relaxed rules about which vineyards can produce them, what types of grapes can be used and so on. Quality Wines, as their full title indicates, have to come from a defined region, and have a long list of other rules covering production factors such as grape varieties, ripeness levels, yields and soils. The way the wine is actually produced and matured may also be specified. Of course these Quality Wines are often, though not always, better than the Table Wines and tend to command a higher price. Within this framework the French classify their wines as follows.

Vin de Table

This is the basic category of French Table Wine. In theory it could come from anywhere in France, and could be made from any grape variety or varieties. No information about region of origin, grape variety or even vintage is allowed on the label. In practice, most Vin de Table comes from southern France, and in particular from the Languedoc-Roussillon region.

Vin de Pays

Vin de Pays (Country Wines) are France's up-market Table Wines. This category was created to offer Vin de Table producers the chance to improve the quality of their wines and sell them for a better price. A Vin de Pays will always tell you whereabouts in France it comes from. Most of the commonly seen names are those of the *départements* (roughly equivalent to English counties) where the grapes grew, e.g. Gard, Hérault and Aude. Vin de Pays can show their varietal composition on the label. Where relevant, a vintage date and the name of the estate where the grapes grew are also allowed on the label. Vin de Pays

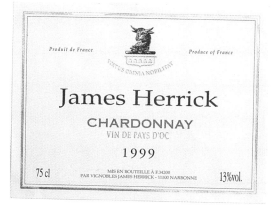

wines have been a big hit with consumers, giving people something that feels like a 'real' wine, at a price only fractionally higher than a Vin de Table. Again, Languedoc-Roussillon is by far the largest producer of these wines.

Vin Délimité de Qualité Supérieure (VDQS)

VDQS is the lower level of quality wine in France. The rules for each VDQS define a production area, permitted soils and grapes, set limits on yields and alcohol levels etc. In theory the rules for VDQS are not as tight as those for AC, but there is very little in it. As time has gone by the VDQS category has become increasingly irrelevant, with most VDQS wines being promoted up to AC.

Appellation d'Origine Contrôlée (AC or AOC)

This is the top-quality category. Above all else, AC defines the production area for a wine. You can imagine that someone has drawn a red line on a map around the permitted vineyards. If your vineyard lies inside the red line, you can sell your wine as, for example, AC Puligny-Montrachet or AC Châteauneuf-du-Pape. If you are outside the red line, tough. Within the permitted area the AC rules will then go on to specify the soils that can be planted. A list of one or more authorised grapes will be laid down. AC Pouilly-Fumé must only be made from Sauvignon Blanc, whereas 13 grape varieties are allowed in the blend for Châteauneuf-du-Pape. Limits are placed on vineyard yields and the wines have to achieve a minimum ABV (to ensure that the grapes were reasonably ripe). Detailed rules may even specify how the vines are to be pruned, and for how long the wines have to be matured.

All AC wines now have to go through a tasting test to check that they reach a minimum quality standard. It would be naïve to think that the tasting test and the other rules guarantee that all AC wines are brilliant. Rather, think of AC as guaranteeing that the wine comes from where it says it does, that it is made to a style that is 'traditional' to the area, and that the wine should at least be free of any glaring faults originating in the vineyard or winery.

Labels showing the four categories of French wine. From left to right: Vin de Table, Vin de Pays, VDQS and AC.

Map labels:

Soulac-sur-Mer

Gironde

MEDOC

St-Estèphe

PREMIERES COTES DE BLAYE

Pauillac
St-Julien

HAUT-MEDOC

Blaye

Listrac
Moulis
Margaux

COTES DE BOURG

Bourg

ST-EMILION SATELLITES

Fronsac
Libourne
Pomerol
St-Emilion

Isle

Bordeaux

PESSAC-LEOGNAN

PREMIERES COTES DE BORDEAUX

Garonne

ENTRE-DEUX-MERS

Dordogne

BERGERAC

Bergerac

Monbazillac

Saussignac

Arcachon

GRAVES

Cérons
Barsac
Cadillac
Loupiac

Ste-Croix-du-Mont

La Réole

Sauterne
Langon

● AC town or village

— AC Bordeaux boundary

Bordeaux

Bordeaux is the world's most famous wine region. It can still justifiably claim to produce more fine wine than anywhere else. That said, it is a large region, with 117,000 ha (292,500 acres) of vineyard. So whilst it does produce some very expensive wines, much of the production is actually un-flashy and moderately priced.

The brilliant success of Bordeaux on the export markets was not achieved overnight. One crucial historical factor, as far as the English-speaking world is concerned, was that the Plantagenet Kings of England ruled Bordeaux for 300 years until 1453. During this period an enormous wine trade developed between Bordeaux and cities like London. The red wine produced in Bordeaux in those days was fairly pale and was called *clairet* in French. It is not surprising, given the awesome linguistic skills of the English, that this very quickly became 'Giz a pint of Claret or I'll rip yer face off'. Of course the term 'Claret' is still with us as a nickname for Bordeaux's red wines.

To be able to produce so many fine wines, there obviously has to be something special about the climate in Bordeaux. The region is located quite a long way south in France, making the climate reasonably warm. It is also right next to the Atlantic Ocean. As well as making Bordeaux a relatively humid region, the ocean has a moderating effect on the climate. The winters are not usually particularly cold, and while the summers are warm, they are not impossibly hot.

AC BORDEAUX

This is the basic appellation covering the whole Bordeaux region. Red, white and rosé versions of AC Bordeaux are made. Much of this wine will sell under merchants' labels (e.g. Barton & Guestier). Where an estate produces and sells one of these wines under the château name (e.g. Château Thieuley), the wine is referred to as a 'petit château'. The AC Bordeaux Supérieur exists for wines that have achieved a higher minimum ABV.

MEDOC AND HAUT-MEDOC

The Médoc is the flat tongue of land lying just north-west of the city of Bordeaux. This area, separating the Atlantic Ocean from the Gironde Estuary, is still in most people's estimation responsible for producing more great red wines than anywhere else in the world. The best soil here is gravel, important for drainage, given that the vineyards are on relatively flat, low-lying land.

The Médoc blend

Most Médoc wines use a blend of grapes:
70% Cabernet Sauvignon (late ripening, concentrated dark fruit aromas, very tannic)
20% Merlot (early ripening, juicy dark fruit aromas, rounder and less tannic)
8% Cabernet Franc (adds some herbal complexity to the blend)
2% Petit Verdot and Malbec.

Fact Box

Typical Médoc blend

70%	Cabernet Sauvignon
20%	Merlot
8%	Cabernet Franc
2%	Petit Verdot and Malbec

Best Buy

Château Cissac, Cru Bourgeois, Médoc 1995

Mid-ruby core. Mid-pink rim. The nose is lifted and intensely cedary. There is plenty of underlying ripe dark fruit. Just the first hint of dry leaves and leather. Dry, mid-acidity, moderate alcohol. Mid-bodied, but with a tight structure. The tannins are still a little on the tough side. Long finish.

Just about approachable now, but it has the fruit and tannin to keep for at least another five to 10 years.

Château Thieuley, one of the most reliable of the scores of AC Bordeaux petits châteaux.

Classifications

Both AC Médoc and AC Haut-Médoc cover red wines only, with the Haut-Médoc judged to produce the finer wines. The appellations go a stage further in the Haut-Médoc, with the top six villages (or 'communes') each having their own appellations: AC St-Estèphe; AC Pauillac; AC St-Julien; AC Margaux; AC Listrac; AC Moulis.

Leading châteaux

Many of Bordeaux's most prestigious châteaux are found in these villages. The good and the great have sat down on various occasions to rate the quality of the wines produced by these estates. League divisions were drawn up to show the relative standing of the top châteaux. The most famous of these classifications was carried out in 1855. The leading 61 châteaux were categorised into five divisions:

Premier (1er) Cru Classé	First Growths
Deuxième (2ème) Cru Classé	Second Growths
Troisième (3ème) Cru Classé	Third Growths
Quatrième (4ème) Cru Classé	Fourth Growths
Cinquième (5ème) Cru Classé	Fifth Growths

(The word 'cru' is best understood as being a vineyard or an estate. The word 'growth' summons up images of polyps and tumours.)

Only five properties sit in the Premier Cru Classé division: Château Lafite; Château Latour; Château Mouton-Rothschild; Château Margaux; Château Haut-Brion.

Châteaux Lafite, Latour and Mouton-Rothschild are all in the commune of Pauillac, so have AC Pauillac on their labels. You do not need a degree in astrophysics to guess that Château Margaux is an AC Margaux. The odd man out is Château Haut-Brion, which actually comes from part of the Graves and sells as AC Pessac-Léognan. Apart from the odd tweak, the 1855 classification has remained unchanged since then. However, if the classification was redone today there would be some promotions and relegations, but the old boys got it just about right 150 years ago.

Second wines

One relatively recent development has been the emergence of 'second wines' from most of the cru classé châteaux. To preserve the quality of their top wines the proprietors and winemakers do a rigorous selection of each year's crop, and the very best vats of wine go into their famous labels. Vats that are good, but not quite good enough to go into the top wine, will then be sold under a second label. For instance, the second wine of Château Latour is 'Les Forts de Latour', while the second wine of Château Lagrange is 'Les Fiefs de Lagrange'.

Cru bourgeois

Classified just beneath the 'cru classé' there are are a number of good properties designated 'cru bourgeois'. These wines are often well worth looking out for as they are reasonably priced relative to their more prestigious neighbours.

Buying 'en primeur'

The selling of fine Bordeaux wines works somewhat differently from most other wines. Rather than maturing, bottling and then releasing a finished wine, top Bordeaux châteaux put their wines on the market just six months after the harvest, whilst the wine is maturing in barrel. At this stage the final blend of the wine will have been completed, but the wine will need another 12 months or so in oak before it is bottled. This system of selling the wine soon after the vintage is known as 'en primeur', with the consumer in effect buying a futures contract.

The advantage for the châteaux is a marked improvement in cash flow. From a consumer point of view there is sometimes an advantage in securing a case or two of a wine when it is first available, assuming the wine subsequently increases in value. Should the wine fall in value, or even worse, a middleman goes bust, then the consumer can lose out.

GRAVES

The Graves district lies south of the city of Bordeaux, along the left bank of the River Garonne. Whereas the various appellations of the Médoc are only for red wines, AC Graves covers both reds and dry whites. In fact, in the past Graves was one of the world's most famous white wines. In recent times dry white Bordeaux wines have struggled in many markets, not least through competition from New World varietal wines. The silver lining from a drinker's point of view is that Bordeaux's dry white wines, Graves included, can now offer good value for money.

Graves in French actually means 'gravel', so the soil is very similar to that encountered in the Médoc. The grape line-up for the red Graves is also the same sort of Cabernet / Merlot blend

seen in the Médoc (Cabernet Sauvignon tends to dominate proceedings on the 'Left Bank' of the Gironde Estuary). The white Graves is usually a blend of around 70% Sémillon and 30% Sauvignon Blanc, with sometimes just a dash of Muscadelle. The proportion of Sauvignon has tended to increase in recent years, not least because Sauvignon gives the wine a more obvious green fruit lift on the nose.

The best of the estates in the Graves, most famously Château Haut-Brion, are tucked in the southern suburbs of the city of Bordeaux. This area was granted its own appellation, Pessac-Léognan, in 1987.

SAUTERNES AND BARSAC

Right down in the southern extremities of the Bordeaux region are the two great sweet white wine appellations, Sauternes and Barsac. Just as AC Médoc was for red wine only, so AC Sauternes and AC Barsac are allowed only for sweet white wines. The grape variety line-up is similar to that found in the Graves, with Sémillon if anything even more dominant (usually around 80% Sémillon and 20% Sauvignon Blanc). It is the thin skin of the Sémillon that makes it susceptible to Noble Rot (*see page 40*). Hence, assuming the autumn weather is favourable, the Sémillon will produce the awesomely sweet and concentrated juice that is the backbone of Sauternes and Barsac.

The Sauvignon Blanc tends to be picked at normal ripeness, and contributes fresh acidity and lively fruit to the final blend. Although nobody knows for certain why this corner of Bordeaux is

Typical white Graves blend

70%	Sémillon
30%	Sauvignon Blanc
	(dash of Muscadelle)

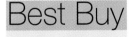

Sauternes, Baron Philippe de Rothschild 1996

Fullish straw-gold appearance. Very distinctive lime marmalade and honey nose. Rich and oily. Sweet, mid-acidity, moderate alcohol. Luscious and ripe. Mid-full bodied. Mid-length. Already drinking well, and will hold for a couple more years.

particularly prone to Noble Rot, the microclimate seems to encourage the development of the *Botrytis cinerea* mould. The increased clay content in the soil compared with the rest of the Graves may be a factor as well.

The leading châteaux in Sauternes and Barsac were classified in 1855, at the same time as the top properties of the Haut-Médoc. The sweet wine classification is slightly different in having Premier Cru Classé and Deuxième Cru Classé categories, but nothing lower. The other quirk is that one estate in Sauternes, Château d'Yquem, was judged to be a cut above the other Premier Cru Classé. As a consequence it is rated as 'Premier Cru Supérieur Classé'.

Château d'Yquem in the autumn, complete with the mist that can trigger Noble Rot.

Clustered around Sauternes and Barsac are several other sweet white wine appellations. They are AC Cérons, AC Ste-Croix-du-Mont, AC Loupiac and also AC Cadillac. Whilst not as concentrated or rich as Sauternes or Barsac, at their very best these can be elegant, sensibly priced, sweet wines.

PREMIERES COTES DE BORDEAUX

This area runs along the east bank of the River Garonne from opposite Sauternes up to the suburbs of Bordeaux. In the past it was best known for its inexpensive medium sweet white wines. As well as these whites, the appellation also covers red wines.

ENTRE-DEUX-MERS

Entre-Deux-Mers literally means 'between the two seas'. The 'seas' in this case are not seas at all, but rather the two large rivers of the Bordeaux region, the Garonne and the Dordogne. The appellation is for dry white wines only. However, the volume of wine produced in this area, both red and white, is large. The red cannot be sold as AC Entre-Deux-Mers, so it will see the light of day as AC Bordeaux or AC Bordeaux Supérieur. The white grape line-up is similar to the Graves.

For the red wines, Merlot has a much more significant role than it had in the Médoc and the Graves areas. There are several reasons why Merlot is good for inexpensive red Bordeaux wine production. Firstly, it ripens about ten days earlier than Cabernet Sauvignon and, secondly, it produces a bigger crop. In addition, it is less tannic than Cabernet Sauvignon and produces wines that are more supple and approachable when young.

ST-EMILION

Although rather busy with tourists, the little medieval town of St-Emilion is probably the prettiest corner of the Bordeaux wine region. The appellation is for red wines only. Merlot is the dominant grape here on the 'Right Bank' of the Gironde, with a typical blend being 65% Merlot, 30% Cabernet Franc and just 5% Cabernet Sauvignon. Whilst there are outcrops of gravel in St-Emilion, many of the commune's finest wines come from the limestone plateau and slope around the town itself. The slightly warmer summer temperatures, combined with the use of the Merlot grape, allow the harvest in St-Emilion to start a week or so earlier than in the Haut-Médoc area. This can be an advantage or disadvantage depending on the weather pattern in September. Certainly the use of the Merlot grape produces wines that are lusher and rounder when young than the sterner and more tannic character of immature 'Left Bank' wines.

Classification

There was no official classification of the St-Emilion châteaux until the 1950s. Unfortunately for the average punter, the system that was introduced is different to that developed 100 years earlier in the Médoc and Sauternes. The hierarchy is as follows:
Premier Grand Cru Classé (A); Premier Grand Cru Classé (B); Grand Cru Classé; Grand Cru.

Fact Box

Typical St-Emilion blend

65%	Merlot
30%	Cabernet Franc
5%	Cabernet Sauvignon

There are only two properties currently rated as Premier Grand Cru Classé (A), Château Ausone and Château Cheval Blanc. One good element of the St-Emilion classification is that the presence of properties in the different categories is reviewed every few years. In other words, châteaux can be promoted and relegated depending on their form.

Garagiste wines

As well as its existing top châteaux, St-Emilion has become famous over the last ten years or so for producing 'garagiste' wines. These are wines that are produced in tiny batches (one of the first was allegedly produced in a garage) from small plots of old vines. These wines tend to be dense, concentrated and impressive to taste. Rave reviews and limited availability have made some of these wines seriously expensive. The fashion now seems to be spreading to other parts of the Bordeaux region, but St-Emilion is the heart of the 'vin de garage' movement.

The satellites

Just outside the boundary of AC St-Emilion are four villages that make wines in a very similar style to their illustrious neighbour. These St-Emilion 'satellites' cannot sell their wines as AC St-Emilion. However, they are allowed to add the word St-Emilion to the name of their own village. Hence you will see around from time to time: AC Lussac-St-Emilion; AC Montagne-St-Emilion; AC St-Georges-St-Emilion; AC Puisseguin-St-Emilion.

These wines are generally moderately priced alternatives to St-Emilion proper. This is a useful fact to bear in mind given the extreme fashionability and high prices commanded by St-Emilion's leading wines.

POMEROL

The tiny village of Pomerol lies between St-Emilion and the town of Libourne. The AC Pomerol is for red wines only, with the Merlot grape making up around 80% of the vineyard area. Parts of Pomerol have a gravelly soil, but there is an outcrop of clay in the north-east of the appellation. Although there is no formal classification, the top wines from the commune sell for as much, and in some cases more, than any other Bordeaux wine. The most famous property in Pomerol is Château Pétrus.

Just as St-Emilion has its satellite villages, so too does Pomerol. The designation for Pomerol's neighbours is AC Lalande-de-Pomerol.

FRONSAC AND CANON-FRONSAC

These two red wine appellations lie immediately to the west of Libourne. The soil here is very rich in lime. As you would expect on the 'Right Bank', Merlot is the dominant grape variety. The wines of Fronsac and Canon-Fronsac have become quite popular as good value-for-money alternatives to St-Emilion.

PREMIERES COTES DE BLAYE AND COTES DE BOURG

Blaye and Bourg lie across the Gironde Estuary from the Haut-Médoc. These appellations cover both reds and dry whites. The wines are straightforward and inexpensive.

BERGERAC

The Bergerac vineyards lie directly to the east of Bordeaux. Although strictly speaking Bergerac is a separate region, the wines are very much in the Bordeaux mould. Much of the wine sells as AC Bergerac, with the dry white and red versions being well distributed. There are various districts within Bergerac that have their own appellations. The most famous of these is AC Monbazillac, a white wine made from Sémillon grapes that have been infected with Noble Rot. AC Saussignac is a similar deliciously sweet white wine.

The famous gravel soil of the Haut-Médoc, seen here in the vineyards of one of St-Estèphe's leading properties, Château Cos d'Estournel.

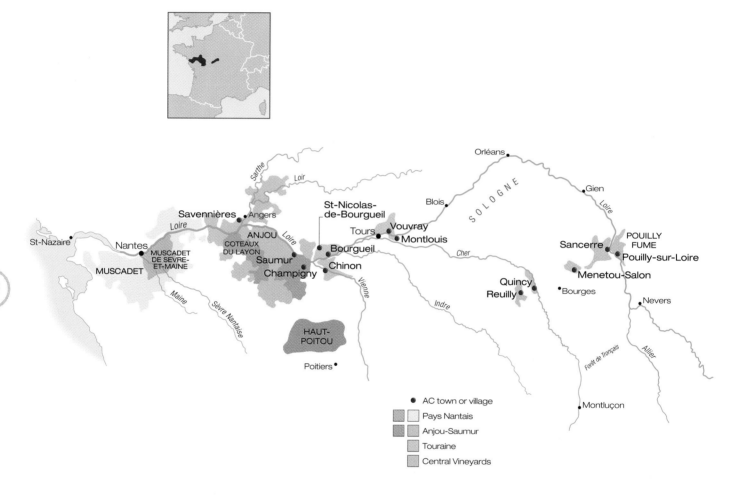

- AC town or village
- Pays Nantais
- Anjou-Saumur
- Touraine
- Central Vineyards

Loire

The gentle but cool climate of the Loire means that the region as a whole is best known for its white wines, though its rosé and sparkling wines also have their followers. Not so often seen outside of France are the Loire's red wines, which actually make up a fair proportion of the production.

The mighty River Loire is almost exactly 1000 km (625 miles) long, from its source in the Cévennes Mountains of southern France to the Atlantic Ocean at St-Nazaire. For the first half of its journey to the sea there are very few vineyards to be seen. However, as the river approaches Orléans it gradually turns to the west and we start to enter wine country. That said, there are few places in the Loire where the vine dominates the landscape in the way that it does in parts of Bordeaux or the Rhône. Rather, the Loire wine region is more a number of relatively small, discreet areas, strung out along the river for several hundred kilometres. What these areas have in common is a relatively cool climate, giving the region's wines a good twang of acidity. This makes them fresh and lively when young. It also allows the best of the sweet wines to keep for a very long time. Indeed the Loire produces some of France's most exhilarating and refreshing white wines.

The Loire wine region is always divided up into four districts, running from west to east: Pays Nantais, Anjou-Saumur, Touraine and the Central Vineyards.

PAYS NANTAIS

This maritime district, centred on the city of Nantes, is famous for just one wine, Muscadet. Bone dry and pretty neutral in character, there was a time around 15 years ago when every wine list in Britain featured Muscadet. Since then, interest has waned, not least perhaps because many drinkers now look for more obvious ripe fruit (and oak) on their white wines. The basic appellation is AC Muscadet. Muscadet is the name not of a village or an area, but of the white grape variety used to make the wine. The most famous sub-district of the Pays Nantais for Muscadet production lies just south-east of Nantes. The two rivers flowing through this area are the Sèvre and the Maine, hence the AC Muscadet de Sèvre et Maine. Although this wine in itself may be no great shakes, it is usually worth paying the extra pennies for a Sèvre et Maine Muscadet rather than a straight version.

What fans of Muscadet should always look out for though is AC Muscadet de Sèvre et Maine Sur Lie. The 'Sur Lie' refers to a trick in the winemaking. Instead of racking the Muscadet off its lees after it has fermented in the autumn, a Sur Lie wine will be left on its lees for at least six months. It is then bottled without filtration. The maturation on the lees gives the wine a lifted, yeasty aroma, and sometimes a slight spritz.

Travellers to France may come across another Pays Nantais white wine, VDQS Gros Plant du Pays Nantais. Searingly acid and raspingly dry, this wine should be tackled only by people who went to boarding school and whose fillings have been checked recently.

ANJOU-SAUMUR

Anjou is best known for its inexpensive medium rosé, AC Rosé d'Anjou, made from a blend of local black grapes (mainly Grolleau). The slightly superior AC Cabernet d'Anjou is the same sort of rosé but this wine is made solely from the Cabernet Franc grape.

The fame of Anjou's rosés has slightly overshadowed the area's white wines. Chenin Blanc is

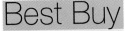

Best Buy

Muscadet de Sèvre et Maine Sur Lie, Château de la Cassemichère 2000

Very pale greenish straw. A few tiny bubbles on the glass. Sharp and tart on the nose. Fairly light intensity. A touch of citrus and earthy breadiness. Dry, high acidity, moderate alcohol. Light-bodied. Lean and lemony flavours on the mid-palate. Shortish finish.

the key white grape. Many of the simpler medium white wines sell as AC Anjou Blanc. Just to the west of the city of Angers is the small, dry white wine appellation of Savennières. AC Savennières is one of the Loire's finest white wines, and is evidence that Chenin Blanc can make world-class dry white wines. Evidence that Chenin Blanc can also make great sweet white wines comes from just opposite Savennières on the south side of the River Loire. AC Coteaux du Layon is made from late-harvested Chenin Blanc, which in top years will have been infected with Noble Rot. There are two tiny appellations within Coteaux du Layon, which produce sweet white wines that are arguably even finer. These are AC Bonnezeaux and AC Quarts-de-Chaume.

Some light and fruity red wines are made from the Cabernet Franc. They will sell as either AC Anjou Rouge or AC Anjou-Villages.

Although the appellation for Saumur includes still wines, the town is most famous for its sparkling wines. Based on Chenin Blanc, these sparkling wines are made by the traditional method. With their tart green fruit character, they can be pleasantly refreshing. However, they lack the complexity of Champagne.

AC Samur-Champigny is a very different beast. Made from Cabernet Franc, Saumur-Champigny and its neighbours in Touraine (AC Chinon, AC Bourgueil and AC St-Nicolas-de-Bourgueil) are the Loire's most serious red wines. Saumur-Champigny from a warm year has an attractive herbal red fruit character. It makes up in elegance what it lacks in brute power.

TOURAINE

For visitors to France, Touraine is the heart of the Loire Valley. This, after all, is where the exquisite châteaux are found: Chambord, Chenonceaux and Azay-le-Rideau to name but three. It is also home to the world's most famous Chenin Blanc, AC Vouvray. The village of Vouvray lies just east of Tours, with the vineyards on a plateau just above the River Loire. Here the soil is 'tufa', a special type of chalk that was boiled by volcanic action. Although it is always a white wine, it does come in a bewildering array of styles: *sec* (dry), *demi-sec* (medium dry), *moelleux* (sweet), *mousseux* (sparkling) and *pétillant* (semi-sparkling). Great sweet Vouvray can be sublime, cheap medium Vouvray can be vile.

Just opposite Vouvray on the south side of the river is AC Montlouis. It makes the same sorts of wine as Vouvray, but is less well known.

Savennières, the small appellation in Anjou that many would say produces the world's finest dry Chenin Blancs.

The other Touraine white wine that has had export success is Sauvignon de Touraine. Crisp and dry, with some of the grassy freshness of the Sauvignon Blanc coming through on the nose, it is one of a number of wines that sell as 'poor man's Sancerre'. The appellation is AC Touraine. Touraine's three specialist red wine appellations lie west of Tours, not far from the Anjou-Saumur border. Chinon lies on the south side of the Loire, Bourgueil and St-Nicolas-de-Bourgueil on the north bank. Like Saumur-Champigny all three are made from the Cabernet Franc. Given the coolness of the climate, these are never going to be massive wines. However, the best examples have charm and harmony, and should not be dismissed just because they are not 14%ABV.

CENTRAL VINEYARDS

Heading east from Touraine the vines fizzle out as the River Loire sweeps to its northernmost point at Orléans. By cutting across the low-lying Sologne you can re-join the river close to the geographical centre of France (hence this wine district's name). On the west bank of the Loire is the hilltop town of Sancerre, with just opposite it on the east bank Pouilly-sur-Loire. AC Sancerre and AC Pouilly-Fumé are enormously popular nowadays and, for many people, represent (along with Marlborough in New Zealand) the world's definitive Sauvignon Blancs. Bone dry and chillingly acid, a good Sancerre or Pouilly-Fumé will balance its austerity with a focused attack of green fruit. Unfortunately, the worst examples are little better than acid rain.

As well as the famous white wines, the Sancerre appellation also covers reds and rosés made from the Pinot Noir. These tend to be light and fruity (and over-priced).

The appearance of Pinot Noir is not so strange as our journey eastwards has got us almost to the gates of Burgundy. However, it is worth being aware of a quirk concerning the wines of Pouilly-sur-Loire. AC Pouilly-Fumé covers the famous wines made from the Sauvignon Blanc, whereas AC Pouilly-sur-Loire is for the simpler dry white wines made from the humble Chasselas grape.

Just south-west of Sancerre are the other areas that make up the Central Vineyards. AC Menetou-Salon, AC Quincy and AC Reuilly all make dry whites from the Sauvignon Blanc grape. The best growers in these appellations can rival their more fêted neighbours in Sancerre and Pouilly-sur-Loire, and usually sell their wines for slightly lower prices. Menetou-Salon and Reuilly also produce some red and rosé wine.

South of the Central Vineyards towards Nevers and Montluçon there are few if any vineyards. However, from a winemaking perspective this is one of the world's most important regions. It is here that several of France's great state oak forests are located. The centuries-old oak trees from these forests (Nevers, Allier, Tronçais) are used to make the finest French oak barrels.

Although not strictly part of the Loire region, the city of Poitiers lies under 100 km (63 miles) to the south of Tours. Nearby are the vineyards of Haut-Poitou. VDQS Sauvignon du Haut-Poitou is a reasonably priced, immediately attractive, dry white wine.

The Vin de Pays du Jardin de la France covers the whole Loire Valley, including Poitiers.

Best Buy

Pouilly-Fumé, Domaine Jean-Claude Chatelain 2000

Pale greenish lemon. Crisp, fresh, moderately intense nose. Sharp green fruit aromas. Apples and gooseberry. Dry, high acidity, moderate alcohol. Light-bodied. A good attack of green fruit. Mid-length on the finish.

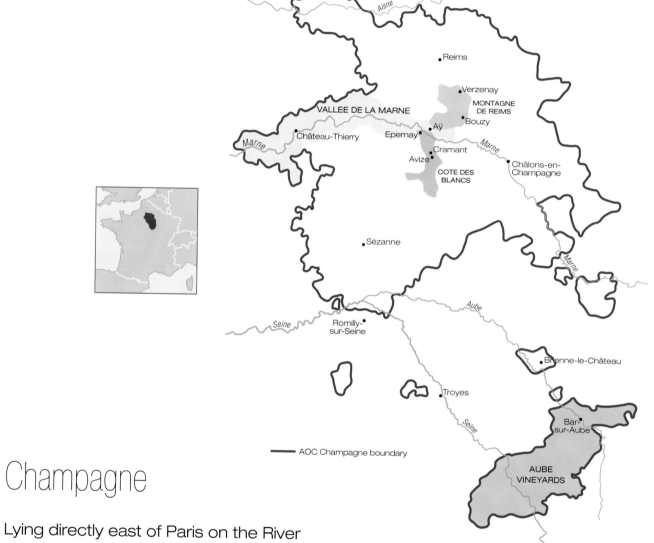

AOC Champagne boundary

Champagne

Lying directly east of Paris on the River
Marne, Champagne is the northernmost
outpost of viticulture in France. Visitors to
these bleak, windswept vineyards in winter
are doubtless surprised that vines can survive
there at all. Yet it is this region that produces
the world's great celebratory drink.

Given the renown of Champagne nowadays, it comes as something of a surprise to discover that the drink that you and I know is a fairly recent invention. Champagne was popular at the court of Louis XIV, but what the Sun King was drinking 300 years ago was a red wine. The concept of sparkling Champagne seems to have been stumbled upon when one winter some barrels of newly fermented Champagne were shipped to England. As the weather warmed up in the spring a second burst of fermentation took place, turning the wine fizzy. Rather than rejecting the stuff, the English took to it with gusto, and exported the fashion back to France. Since then the process of generating the sparkle in bottle has been worked out, refined and largely automated.

Technical issues aside, Champagne has been brilliantly marketed. Anything with a whiff of celebration or style about it, horse and motor racing, the opera, ship launches, you name it, the Champagne boys will be there. Yet underneath the polished exterior the wine still has to be produced from grapes grown in one of the world's coolest and most treacherous vineyard regions.

Harsh climate and chalk soil

The great positive of Champagne's chilly, marginal climate is that the grapes grown there will always be high in acidity. This searing backbone of acidity contributes much to the wine's finesse and longevity. Spring frost, hail and harvest rain are the negatives of such a northern location.

The AC Champagne delimited area covers 35,000 ha (87,500 acres) of land, nearly all of which is now planted with vines.

The subsoil in Champagne is solid chalk. Chalk is sometimes described as being a very intelligent subsoil. Water can drain into the chalk very quickly, ensuring that the vineyard never becomes waterlogged. However, the rock itself will hold on to some of the moisture. During the summer the vine's roots can reach down into the chalk and drawn off this water. It is also relatively easy to

The stark beauty of Champagne in winter.

The world of wine

tunnel into the chalk, creating the caves where the Champagne will mature. The actual layer of soil on top of the chalk is very shallow. In the past the main fertiliser used was minced-up bin bag garbage. This has stopped now, so the irony (or not) of the world's most decadent wine being grown on filth is no more.

The varietals

Betraying its red wine origins, three-quarters of the Champagne vineyards are planted with black grapes. The black varieties are Pinot Noir and Pinot Meunier. The only white variety grown in the region is Chardonnay. These varieties each have their own prime vineyard locations. What is more, although they are grown in different districts of the region, most Champagnes will be produced by blending wines made from the three grape varieties. Each grape is reckoned to contribute something to the overall blend.

The Pinot Noir grows on the Montagne de Reims and gives most Champagnes their structure and backbone. The Pinot Meunier is found in the Vallée de la Marne and contributes an immediate fruitiness (important in Champagnes that are going to be drunk young). The Côte des Blancs is where the Chardonnay is planted. Chardonnay is reckoned to give the finished Champagne its finesse and elegance. There is a southern outpost of the Champagne region by the River Aube. This area is mainly planted with Pinot Noir.

From grapes to bubbles

Contrary to what you might expect, the majority of Champagne's vineyards are not owned by the large Champagne companies. The grape growing is primarily done by individual farmers. Many of these sell their grapes to the big Champagne houses. Some growers are members of co-operative wineries, whilst others actually make and market their own Champagnes.

Picking and pressing

All the grapes in Champagne are picked by hand. Rather than having to truck the grapes to the big wineries, which are mainly located in Reims and Epernay, there are press houses located in many of the grape growing villages. The pressing has to be done very carefully, not least to ensure that no colour is released from the skins of the Pinot Noir and Pinot Meunier grapes. Only two pressings are allowed in Champagne production. The juice from the first pressing is the 'cuvée' and that from the second is the 'taille'.

Blending the base wines

Once the colourless juice has been obtained it is taken to the winery, allowed to settle and then fermented like any other dry white wine. The resulting base wine is pretty austere, being bone dry, rather thin and screamingly high in acidity. The challenge for the winemaker is to taste, analyse and assess the various base wines at his disposal. At the bigger Champagne houses the winemaker may be working with hundreds of different base wines. Some will be Pinot Noir, some will be Pinot Meunier and some will be Chardonnay. Some of the Pinot Noir may be from the village of Verzenay, some from Bouzy, some from Aÿ. Of the Pinot Noir from Aÿ, some may

Champagne Charles Heidsieck Brut Non-Vintage, Mis en Cave 1996

Very good *mousse*. Palish straw. Intensely yeasty on the nose. The fruit is reminiscent of grapefruit and apple. There is a buttery, biscuity note as well. Dry, very high acidity, moderate alcohol. Mid-bodied. Crisp and lively. Just a hint of minerality starting to develop. Long finish.

have been picked on 20th September, some on 22nd September and some on 26th September. Some will be *cuvée* and some will be *taille*.

Non-Vintage Champagne

From this bewildering array of options the wine-maker has to decide what is to be blended with what to obtain each style of Champagne. The bread and butter of most Champagne producers is their Non-Vintage wine. A blend is put together based on the current year's wines. Crucially though, older reserve wines from previous years are added to the blend. There are good reasons for using the reserve wines. Firstly, given the unpredictability and variability of the weather in Champagne, the use of reserve wines allows a producer to smooth out any huge changes of flavour or quality between one year's production and the next. Secondly, being older, the reserve wines add maturity to the overall blend. Thirdly, the top Non-Vintage Champagnes contain a selection of reserve wines from a number of different years. In this way complexity is added to the blend.

The stark beauty of Champagne in spring (no back chat, this is the commissioning editor's favourite photograph).

Remuage drives the yeast sediment down to the neck of the bottle.

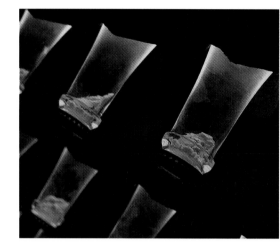

Vintage Champagne

If the weather was good during the year in question, the winemaker may have spotted several base wines that were particularly impressive. He will blend these, but not add any reserve wines. This blend from just one year will be a Vintage Champagne. Most Champagne houses also produce limited amounts of what is called 'Prestige Cuvée' Vintage Champagne. This is a selection of the very finest base wines, made in the same way as a Vintage Champagne, but usually packaged in a fancy bottle and sold for an even more fancy price.

White, black and pink

If a blend is put together using only Chardonnay, the resulting Champagne will be described as a 'Blanc de Blancs' (a white wine made from white grapes). Occasionally you may come across a 'Blanc de Noirs' Champagne, where the blend consisted of Pinot Noir and Pinot Meunier only.

As far as rosé Champagnes are concerned, some are produced in the same way as a regular still rosé wine – in other words, by leaving the crushed black grapes with their skins for a few hours. However, most are made by the easier route of putting a normal base wine blend together, then adding a dash of red wine to obtain the pink colour.

Introducing bubbles

Having completed the blending, there is the small matter of getting the bubbles into the Champagne. A mixture of sugar and yeast (*liqueur de tirage*) is added to the base wine blend. The wine is then bottled (the closure at this stage being a 'crown cork' – a glorified beer bottle top). The bottles are taken down into the caves and stacked on their sides. Inside each bottle the yeast will attack the sugar and there will be a second burst of fermentation. The alcohol content will go up to around 12%ABV, but more importantly the carbon dioxide generated will turn the Champagne fizzy. The pressure in each bottle goes up to around 6 atmospheres. The heaviness of the glass in a Champagne bottle is necessary to resist this pressure. The second fermentation in the bottle is quite slow because of the coolness of the caves, around 12°C (54°F). It takes about three months for all the sugar to be used up. The yeast then die and form a sediment on the side of the bottle.

Maturing the wine

The bottles are left where they are in the caves to mature. Much of the flavour of a Champagne comes from this maturation on the yeast. A complex exchange of compounds takes place

Dosage (sugar) level descriptions

Extra Brut
Brut
Extra Sec
Sec
Demi-Sec
Doux

between the wine and yeast as the latter digest themselves (a process called 'yeast autolysis') – a useful fact to know next time you are struggling to account for the odd aroma of the Champagne you are sipping from an actress's slipper! The appellation law for Champagne specifies that all Non-Vintage Champagnes have to mature on the yeast for at least 15 months. Vintage Champagnes have to mature for at least three years. It is worth saying that most of the top Champagne houses mature their wines for much longer than these legal minima.

Remuage

Once fully mature, the yeast have to be removed from the bottle. This is achieved in two stages. *Remuage* involves loading the bottles horizontally into a rack called a pupitre, then over a period of several weeks the bottles are turned and tipped up a little every day. At the end of this process the bottles will be nearly vertical, cork down, with the yeast stuck up against the cork. The Stakhanovite *remueurs* reckon they can turn 50,000 bottles a day. This is still not good enough given France's high labour costs, so most of the *remuage* is now automated using 'gyropalettes'. These computer-controlled metal cages, loaded with bottles, turn several times a day and achieve the *remuage* in a few days.

Dégorgement and dosage

With the *remuage* completed, the bottles then undergo *dégorgement*. The bottles, still neck down, are plunged into a bath of freezing salt water. This freezes a small plug of wine in the neck of the bottle, trapping the yeast. The bottle can then be turned upright and the cork removed. The 6 atmospheres of pressure in the bottle fire out the plug of ice containing the yeast.

The small volume of wine lost in this way is replaced by topping up the bottle with *liqueur d'expédition*. This is reserve wine to which cane sugar has been added. The more sugar that is dissolved in the *liqueur d'expédition*, the sweeter the Champagne will be (of course it is normally illegal to sweeten a wine by adding sugar). The amount of sugar that is added is called the 'dosage'. It is quite confusing that even 'Brut' (theoretically, very dry) Champagne will have received a small dosage. However, given the very high underlying acidity of Champagne, it is generally accepted that most Champagnes need a little sugar present to provide balance.

Once topped-up the cork is driven in and wired down. The bottle is shaken to mix in the *liqueur d'expédition*. The whole *dégorgement*, topping up and corking process takes a matter of seconds, so the loss of pressure from the bottle is marginal. Many producers will then let the bottle rest for a few weeks or months before labelling and dispatch.

Still Champagne

Although the Champagne region is renowned the world over for its sparkling wine, a little bit of still wine is produced (both dry white and red). This still wine cannot sell as AC Champagne. Instead it has its own appellation, Coteaux Champenois. These still wines are rather lean and austere (and quite pricey for what they are).

Fact Box

Champagne is famous for its large format bottles. Here is the family:

Quarter	20cl
Half	37.5cl
Bottle	75cl
Magnum	150cl
Jereboam	300cl
Rehoboam	450cl
Methuselah	600cl
Salmanazar	900cl
Balthasar	1200cl
Nebuchadnezzar	1500cl

Alsace

This magical region lies in the north-east of France, separated from Germany by the River Rhine. Many aspects of life and culture in Alsace have a fascinating hybrid nature, part French, part German. The German influence is seen particularly strongly in the names of the villages, vineyards, family names and architecture.

Being so far north in France gives Alsace a distinctly cool climate. This makes it very much white wine territory, with under 10% of the region's production being red and rosé. The other huge influence on the climate of Alsace are the Vosges mountains, peaking at just under 1500 m (4921 ft), and cutting off Alsace from the rest of France. The Vosges form a formidable barrier to the rain-bearing clouds tracking across France from the Atlantic Ocean. The result is that Alsace ends up with a freakishly dry climate. The town of Colmar in the centre of the Alsace vineyards has the same sort of rainfall as cities on the Mediterranean such as Narbonne. Blessed with this cool, dry continental climate, Alsace can ripen its grapes late into the autumn, largely protected from the harvest rains that can be such a problem in regions like the Loire.

A complex soil

Alsace probably has the most complex mix of soil types of any of France's vineyard regions. The geological upheavals that created the Vosges mountains brought many layers of strata to the surface within a very small area. Four vineyards within the same village might have clay-, limestone-, granite- and sandstone-based soils respectively. The vineyards of Alsace are on the lower slopes of the Vosges, with the best sites usually facing south or south-east.

Wine styles

Most of the white wines in Alsace were fermented to dryness in the past. Quite a few are now bottled with just a hint of sweetness, off-dry rather than medium dry. As well as these normal white wines, Alsace does make small amounts of late-harvested wine. 'Vendange Tardive' wines are made by leaving the grapes on the vine even later into the autumn than usual. The resulting high sugar level in the grapes can give either a wine that is dry but higher in alcohol and richer than normal, or, if the yeast are unable to ferment all the sugar, a medium or sweet wine. In really special years some of these late-harvested grapes will have been infected with Noble Rot. This will have pushed the sugar content in the grapes to heroic levels, allowing the production of lusciously sweet wines called 'Sélection de Grains Nobles'.

Classification

Compared with the complexities encountered in other parts of France, the appellation system in Alsace is a cinch. The vast majority of wines are covered by the simple AC Alsace. One of the rules laid down in the appellation is that the wines have to be bottled in the Alsace region, using a green flute bottle (*flûte d'Alsace*). This is a mixed blessing. In France, where very little German wine is sold, the Alsace bottles stand out clearly on the shelves of supermarkets and wine shops. In the UK, it is very easy for the Alsace wines to get mixed up with German or even Slovenian wines. Given the dire image of German wine in Britain at the moment, this confusion probably does Alsace no favours at all.

The top 50 vineyards in Alsace are entitled to the superior designation, AC Alsace Grand Cru. The small amount of sparkling wine produced in the region (by the traditional method) is covered by AC Crémant d'Alsace.

Alsace varietals

Having a simple appellation system is no bad thing, given the range of grape varieties that are grown in Alsace. The vast majority are sold as single varietal wines. The varietal rules are very strict in Alsace. If you label a wine as Gewurztraminer, 100% of the liquid in the bottle has to be Gewurztraminer.

Gewurztraminer
This for many people is the signature wine of Alsace. The exotic, floral aromas and opulent mouthfeel are something you either adore or despise. Alsace Gewurztraminer is famed for its ability to partner powerfully flavoured dishes such as smoked fish and some Chinese specialities.

Riesling
The antithesis of Gewurztraminer, Alsace Riesling is austere and minerally, with a taut backbone of acidity. Unlike Gewurztraminer, a top Riesling can age gracefully in the bottle and develop great complexity. The dry Alsace Rieslings are a perfect accompaniment for trout.

Edelzwicker
Not a grape variety at all, Edelzwicker means 'noble blend'. This is usually a simple, glugging dry white wine, often produced by pepping up some Pinot Blanc or Sylvaner with a dollop of Gewurztraminer or Pinot Gris.

Muscat
Scented and citrusy on the nose, Muscat d'Alsace is usually fermented dry. In Alsace it is often drunk as an apéritif.

Pinot Blanc
Pinot Blanc is now the region's main workhorse grape. It produces wines with an immediate fruitiness, which are relatively light on the palate.

Sylvaner
Terribly unfashionable at the moment, Sylvaner is often a bit neutral and thin. Drunk young though, it can be clean and refreshing.

Pinot Noir
The odd man out, Pinot Noir is responsible for some light-bodied reds and rosés.

Pinot Gris
In the past this was often labelled as 'Tokay d'Alsace' and even today the name 'Tokay-Pinot Gris' is still used. Alsace Pinot Gris is often rich and full on the palate, with a broad, honeyed, sometimes almost spicy nose. Given the paucity of red wine in Alsace, Pinot Gris is often pressed into service to partner game such as wild boar and venison.

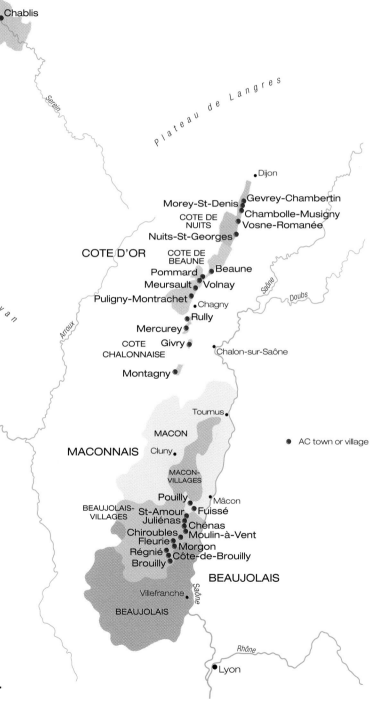

Chablis

Auxerre

Plateau de Langres

Dijon

Morey-St-Denis   Gevrey-Chambertin
COTE DE   Chambolle-Musigny
NUITS   Vosne-Romanée
Nuits-St-Georges

COTE D'OR
COTE DE
BEAUNE
Pommard   Beaune
Meursault   Volnay
Puligny-Montrachet
Chagny

Rully
Mercurey
COTE   Givry
CHALONNAISE   Chalon-sur-Saône

Montagny

Tournus

MACON

MACONNAIS   Cluny

MACON-
VILLAGES   • AC town or village

Pouilly   Mâcon
BEAUJOLAIS-   St-Amour   Fuissé
VILLAGES   Juliénas   Chénas
Chiroubles   Moulin-à-Vent
Fleurie
Régnié   Morgon
Brouilly   Côte-de-Brouilly

BEAUJOLAIS

Villefranche

BEAUJOLAIS

Lyon

Burgundy

Even for relatively knowledgeable wine drinkers, Burgundy has been, until very recently, a notoriously difficult region to get to grips with. However, despite the terrifying prices and the horrendously complicated structure of the vineyards in Burgundy, consumers world-wide are now much more familiar with the sublime quality of the region's top wines.

Burgundy and Bordeaux are France's two most prestigious wine regions. Yet in character they are completely different. In part these differences were shaped by their very different medieval histories. Given its dynastic and trading links with England, Bordeaux came to be the benchmark red wine of the English-speaking world. By contrast, Burgundy's links were with the royal court in Paris and the Low Countries.

In terms of latitude Burgundy is further north than Bordeaux and so therefore has a cooler climate. What is more, lying inland, Burgundy has a much less maritime climate. Temperatures are more extreme, with cold winters and some very hot days in the summer. Spring frost is always a particular worry in Chablis and the Côte d'Or.

AC BOURGOGNE

AC Bourgogne is the appellation that covers virtually the whole Burgundy region ('Burgundy' is the anglicised name for 'Bourgogne'). Red and dry white versions of AC Bourgogne are amongst the most affordable of Burgundy's wines, although there really is no such thing as inexpensive Burgundy.

CHABLIS

Chablis is one of the world's most elegant dry white wines. It is made from the Chardonnay grape, and fans would say it is the purest expression of this variety. Of course today Chardonnay is planted in almost every wine producing country on earth. So what makes Chablis special? The first distinguishing feature of Chablis is its taut, austere backbone of acidity. This is a function of the extreme northern position of the vineyards, only 170 km (106 miles) south-east of Paris. The Burgundians are the most fanatical followers of the *terroir* cult, so there is going to be something special about the soil. In Chablis it is a chalky clay containing fossilised oysters ('kimmeridgian clay'). One other feature of Chablis is that most of it is not aged in oak. This allows the austere fruit character to come through, and is in marked contrast to the oaky Chardonnays from the New World.

Terroir, AC ratings and classifications

The importance of *terroir* to the Burgundians is borne out by the way each individual vineyard in the region is treated as a unique entity. In fact the

Best Buy

Chablis Grand Cru 'Les Clos', J. Moreau et Fils 1997

Mid-greenish lemon. Focused and pure on the nose. Green and white fruit notes: apple, pear and melon. Just a hint of butteriness. Dry, highish acidity, mid-alcohol. Nutty and rounded. Mid-bodied. Fairly long finish.

91

Burgundy

The three-stage hierarchy used for the finest Burgundies. From left to right: a 'straight' village Puligny-Montrachet, a Premier Cru and a Grand Cru.

AC ratings in Chablis

AC Chablis
Where a wine carries just the name of the village, it will come from vineyards on flatter, less favourable land.

AC Chablis Grand Cru
Forget it, you can't afford it. The 'Grand Cru' vineyards are positioned on the best slopes and produce the most concentrated wines. As with the Premiers Crus, the Grands Crus will give the name of the field on the label e.g. Bougros, Blanchot and Valmur.

AC Chablis Premier Cru
The 'Premier Cru' tells you that the wine comes from a superior-quality vineyard, located on a slope. Most Premier Cru wines will tell you the actual name of the vineyard where the grapes grew. Examples in Chablis include Fourchaume, Monts de Milieu, Montmains and Vaillons.

Best Buy

Beaune Premier Cru, Louis Jadot 1996

Mid-garnet core. Mid-broad garnet rim.Pure, cool red fruit aromas are very much to the fore: redcurrant and red cherry. Just starting to develop some leathery, peaty notes.Dry, mid-acidity, mid-high alcohol. Mid-light bodied. A decent grip of firm tannins. Good fruit on the mid-palate. Longish finish.Just starting to drink well now, but will easily keep for five years or more.

top Burgundies actually tell you the name of the field they come from. Each of these fields has an Appellation Contrôlée rating. The system is easiest to understand in the context of Chablis (*see chart above*). As if the village / Premier Cru / Grand Cru rating system for each field were not enough, there is one final element of complexity that will have you reaching for the gin bottle (if you haven't already!). Because of the division of the Burgundy vineyards after the French Revolution, and the workings of the French inheritance law, most of the fields in Burgundy are actually sub-divided amongst a number of individual growers. So what might look like a single block of land to you and me, is actually divided up like an allotment or a patchwork quilt. Each of the growers in a vineyard is allowed to produce wine and sell it under the vineyard name. In this way you can get 20 or 30 different versions of some Premiers and

Grands Crus. Coming from prestigious vineyards they should all be pretty good, but unfortunately this is not always the case. A lot depends on how carefully the vines were nurtured by each grower, and the expertise employed in the winemaking.

One result of this is that when it comes to buying Burgundy it often pays to stick with growers or merchants whose wines you like, rather than automatically chasing after something that comes from a famous village or vineyard.

COTE D'OR
This is the heart of Burgundy. The Côte d'Or (or 'Golden Slope') is a gentle south-east facing slope that runs for about 50 km (31 miles) from Dijon down past Beaune, petering out near Chagny. It is responsible for producing the world's most prestigious dry white wines, and the most delicate and exquisite red wines. All the great white Burgundies are made from Chardonnay. All the great red Burgundies are made from Pinot Noir. Limestone is the underlying rock. So far, so good. Being Burgundy, the differentiation between wines is going to come from the *terroir*. As in Chablis, the exact aspect, drainage and soil composition will determine whether a field produces village, Premier Cru or Grand Cru wine.

Côte de Nuits
The Côte d'Or is divided into the Côte de Nuits and the Côte de Beaune. The Côte de Nuits is almost entirely devoted to red wine. The most famous villages are Gevrey-Chambertin, Morey-St-Denis, Chambolle-Musigny, Vosne-Romanée and Nuits-St-Georges (from which the Côte de

Nuits takes its name). Individual Grand Cru vineyards to look out for if you win the lottery include Le Chambertin, Le Musigny, Clos de Vougeot, La Tâche and Romanée-Conti. The 2 ha (5 acres) that make up the Romanée-Conti vineyard produce the world's most expensive red wine.

Côte de Beaune

The Côte de Beaune is more evenly divided between red and white wine. Communes like Volnay, Pommard and Beaune itself primarily stick with the Pinot Noir and therefore make red wines. These reds tend to be more open textured and

The gentle slopes of the Côte d'Or, holy ground for lovers of Burgundy.

The world of wine

forward than the wines of the Côte de Nuits. Just south of the village of Volnay there is a change in soil composition that favours the Chardonnay over the Pinot Noir. Hence the villages of Meursault and Puligny-Montrachet are devoted to white wine production. Between them these two villages make the world's most complex and harmonious dry white wines. The Côte de Beaune's Grand Cru whites include Le Montrachet, Chevalier-Montrachet and Corton-Charlemagne.

Beaune

The walled, medieval city of Beaune is the centre of the Burgundy wine trade. Although nowadays many growers in Burgundy produce, bottle and sell their own wines, a large number of the smaller growers just do not have the resources to vinify, mature, bottle and market their wines themselves. This is where the *négociants* (merchants) have an important role to play. They will buy grapes, juice or wine from individual growers, vinify and/or mature the wine (and if necessary blend it with other parcels of wine from the same village or vineyard), bottle it and then market the wine around the world.

COTE CHALONNAISE

After the profound quality and terrifying prices of the Côte d'Or, the Côte Chalonnaise represents a return to normality (and affordability). As with its august northerly neighbour, the reds are made from Pinot Noir and most of the whites from Chardonnay. The appellations for Mercurey, Givry and Rully cover both reds and dry whites, whereas Montagny is restricted to dry whites.

The Côte Chalonnaise does make some dry white wines from a white grape called the Aligoté. This rather austere, acidic, dry white wine usually sells as AC Bourgogne Aligoté. A 'Kir' is traditionally made by adding a dash of liqueur de cassis (blackcurrant liqueur) to Bourgogne Aligoté.

There is also some sparkling wine made in the Côte Chalonnaise (and the Maconnais) using the traditional method. This has the appellation Crémant de Bourgogne.

MACONNAIS

AC Mâcon covers the relatively humble wines from this district of Burgundy. Chardonnay remains the key white grape. However, given that Beaujolais lies immediately to the south, it is perhaps not surprising that the Gamay grape should take over as the principal black variety. The better white wine producing villages have the right to sell their wines as AC Mâcon-Villages. In fact, if the wine comes from just one of these communes, the word 'Villages' can be dropped and replaced with the actual village name e.g. Mâcon-Lugny. The top white wine vineyards in the Maconnais have their own appellation, Pouilly-Fuissé.

BEAUJOLAIS

Beaujolais is famous the world over for its soft, fruity, glugging red wines. By Burgundy standards Beaujolais is enormous, accounting for over half of the region's wine production. Many aspects of Beaujolais production are quite different to the rest of Burgundy. Gamay, rather than Pinot Noir, is the grape variety grown in Beaujolais. The best soils in the area are based on granite rather than limestone. Even the training system (*see page 37*) is different, with *Gobelet* used in Beaujolais as opposed to the *Guyot* or *Cordon de Royat* used in the Côte d'Or. Also, being the southernmost district in Burgundy, the climate is relatively warm.

Nouveau and Crus

AC Beaujolais is the basic appellation. Most of this simplest of all Beaujolais is produced in the south of the district, just outside Lyon. These vineyards also produce most of the AC Beaujolais Nouveau. By using *macération carbonique* (*see page 59*) the wineries are able to turn grapes into bottled wine in under eight weeks. The release day is always the third Thursday in November. Nowadays we are quite blasé about its release, but in the 1980s, the annual release of Beaujolais Nouveau was a huge event, with the wine arriving by helicopter, parachute and Bentley, as well as lorry.

Thirty-eight of the better villages in the northern half of the area are allowed to sell their wines as AC Beaujolais-Villages.

Top of the hierarchy in Beaujolais are the ten villages that have the right to their very own appellations. They are often referred to as the 'Beaujolais Crus'. The ten are: Brouilly, Chénas, Chiroubles, Côte de Brouilly, Fleurie, Juliénas, Morgon, Moulin-à-Vent, Régnié and St-Amour. Moulin-à-Vent is generally reckoned to be the most concentrated and structured, the nearest thing to 'serious' Beaujolais. The best examples can be cellared for a few years, rather than drunk within minutes of purchase. The Cru Beaujolais tend to be vinified like classic red wines, rather than produced by using *macération carbonique*.

JURA

The beautiful mountainous Jura region along France's border with Switzerland is only a small producer of wine. However, what it lacks in volume it makes up for in a bewildering proliferation of styles. Reds, whites, rosés and sparkling wines are made from both familiar (Pinot Noir, Chardonnay, Pinot Blanc) and obscure (Trousseau, Poulsard, Savagnin) grape varieties. The main appellations are Arbois and Côtes du Jura.

The region also makes two speciality white wines. Vin Jaune ('yellow wine') is a dry white wine that has matured in barrel under a layer of 'flor' yeast (just like Fino Sherry – *see page 134*). This style of pungent dry white wine can keep for an extremely long time. The most famous example of Vin Jaune is AC Château Chalon, although both AC Arbois and AC Côtes du Jura can be made in this style. Vin de Paille ('straw wine') is a sweet white wine made from grapes that have been dried indoors (originally on straw mats). Like Vin Jaune it normally sells under the Arbois or Côtes du Jura appellations.

SAVOIE

Precious little wine is exported from this mountainous region near Geneva, not least because production volumes are small. Reds, dry whites, rosés and sparkling wines are produced. As in the Jura, local grapes like Mondeuse, Altesse and Jacquère rub shoulders with Gamay, Pinot Noir, Chardonnay, Aligoté and Chasselas. The main Appellation Contrôlée wines are Vin de Savoie, Crépy and Seyssel, with Bugey being a VDQS.

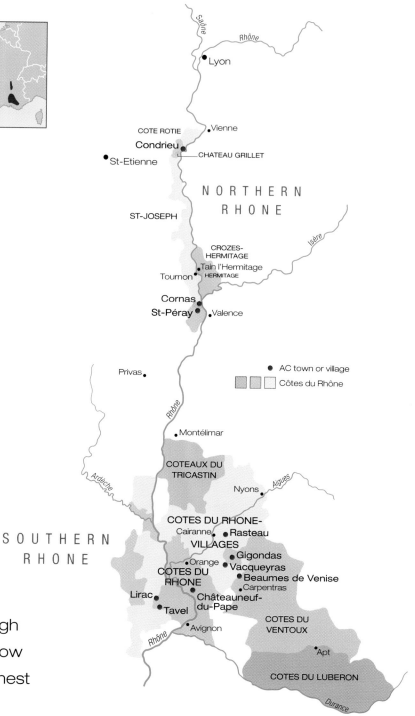

Rhône

For much of the twentieth century it was the quantitative side of the Rhône that most people were aware of, rather than the qualitative potential. That has all changed over the last decade or so. As well as fetching high prices, the Rhône's top wines are now respected as being some of the richest and most intense in the world.

Once the River Rhône has reached Lyon it turns to the south and barely falters on its course to the Mediterranean. With a relatively warm and dry climate it is logical that the region should primarily be a producer of red wines. The one freak climatic phenomenon that the growers have to contend with is the 'Mistral'. This cold northerly wind blows down the valley from time to time. It can break off tender vine shoots in some of the exposed vineyards of the northern Rhône. That said, in some damp years, the drying effect of the Mistral can help keep Grey Rot at bay.

Geology, above all else, divides the Rhône's vineyards into two very unequal halves.

NORTHERN RHONE

Just south of Lyon the River Rhône enters a narrow gorge, formed by millions of years of erosion of the hard granitic rocks. Most of the northern Rhône's great wines come from terraced vineyards cut into this granite. Production is inevitably small, the whole northern Rhône contributing only around 5% to the regional total. The cultivation costs are obviously high as most, if not all, of the vineyard work has to be done by hand. The key grape variety of the northern Rhône is the Syrah. Running from north to south the appellations are as follows.

AC Côte Rôtie

Côte Rôtie is the world's most elegant Syrah wine. Generally less bruising than Hermitage, Côte Rôtie can show a perfumed, violet-scented side of the Syrah grape. Although Syrah is the dominant black variety, many growers do still add to the fermentation vats a small proportion (around 5%) of the white grape Viognier. There are two main slopes in Côte Rôtie, the Côte Brune and the Côte Blonde (named after the differing soil colours). Because of the risk of damage by the Mistral, the vines on some of the steepest slopes of Côte Rôtie are trained up posts in a 'wigwam' fashion.

AC Condrieu and AC Château Grillet

This is the finest dry white wine produced in the Rhône Valley. Condrieu is the home of the Viognier grape variety, and it remains its apotheosis. There are few reasons for living in our sad degraded age; Condrieu is one of them. To the neophyte the aroma of Condrieu can come as quite a shock. Intensely aromatic and rich, there is often an almost overwhelming apricot skin character to the nose. The palate is full and lush, with low acidity and high alcohol. Even today, given the cult status of Viognier, the vineyard area of Condrieu is only just over 100 ha (250 acres). Prices are high. Château Grillet is a tiny appellation within Condrieu, again using the Viognier grape to produce a rich but dry white wine.

AC St-Joseph

The appellation area for St-Joseph overlaps with that for Condrieu in the north, then runs down the west side of the Rhône for about 50 km (31 miles). The area of land under vine is only 900 ha (2250 acres). The reds are based on Syrah and offer good value for money in what has become a pricey region. The dry whites are pleasant and are made from a blend of Marsanne and Roussanne.

FRANCE

Château Grillet and Condrieu, the steep terraced vineyards from which Viognier's conquest of the world was launched.

AC Hermitage

For many people red Hermitage remains the quintessential Syrah and the Rhône Valley's greatest wine. Opaque in colour when young, the nose and palate can be dense and unyielding. With age though a glorious complex bouquet develops and the palate becomes warm and smooth. A small amount of dry white Hermitage wine is made from the Marsanne and Roussanne. The vineyards themselves consist of a steep

south-facing slope on the east side of the river, which is directly above the small town of Tain l'Hermitage.

AC Crozes-Hermitage

The less well-sited vineyards near Tain l'Hermitage have the appellation Crozes-Hermitage. Whilst not a patch on Hermitage proper, Crozes-Hermitage in both its red and dry white guises can be very good value for money. The grape line-up is the same as for Hermitage.

AC Cornas

Back on the west side of the river and a short distance south is the village of Cornas. This full-bodied red, made from Syrah as usual, used to be something of a bargain. No more. That said, it is an impressive wine that can age well, like Hermitage and Côte Rôtie.

AC St-Péray

This appellation produces some relatively simple dry white wines, both still and sparkling. Marsanne and Roussanne are the grape varieties employed.

SOUTHERN RHONE

St-Péray lies just opposite the town of Valence, and from there down past Montélimar there is a 50 km (31 mile) gap with very few vines (but plenty of nuclear reactors). Eventually the Rhône Valley broadens out and as you approach Orange the vine returns to dominate the landscape. Most of the vineyards in the southern Rhône are located on relatively flat land, often with a stony soil formed when the Rhône glacier retreated. A blend of black grapes is normally used in the southern Rhône. Grenache tends to be the dominant player, with contributions from Cinsault, Mourvèdre and Syrah. The climate in the southern Rhône is that bit warmer than the north, with some very high temperatures recorded in the summer. All these factors together produce red wines that are a bit rounder and spicier than the aristocrats from 'up north'. The key appellations in the southern Rhône are as follows.

AC Côtes du Rhône

This is your classic 'Two pints of Côtes du Rhône and a packet of crisps, please'. The appellation covers the whole Rhône Valley, north and south, but in practice it is the sprawl of vineyards around Orange that makes most of the Côtes du Rhône. A decent Côtes du Rhône is soft and good value for money. Sadly – not surprising given the volume produced – there is also a lot of utter swill. Red Côtes du Rhône is the main style produced, but a little rosé and dry white are also made.

AC Côtes du Rhône-Villages

You can regard this appellation as being a thinking man's Côtes du Rhône. Reds, whites and rosés are all permitted but, as you would expect, the former predominates. The best 16 villages are allowed to add the actual name of their village to the 'Côtes du Rhône-Villages'. For example, one of the top villages is Cairanne, and the wines from there often sell as AC Côtes du Rhône-Villages Cairanne. There are another 70 villages that can use the AC Côtes du Rhône-Villages, but they are not allowed to add the name of their commune.

Best Buy

St Joseph, Cave de Tain l'Hermitage 1999

Very dark blackish ruby. Narrow pink-purple rim. The nose is dense and solid. Whiffs of tar, white pepper and violets. Plenty of underlying black fruit. Dry, lowish acidity, fairly high alcohol. Mid-full bodied. Fairly tannic, but there is a ripeness to the tannins. Dark fruits and a savoury meaty note as well. Mid-length. Serve at room temperature.

Just about approachable now. Two or three years of further ageing will smooth out the tannins.

'Wigwam' training of Syrah vines at Côte Rôtie.

The world of wine

AC Châteauneuf-du-Pape

The most famous village in the southern Rhône to have its own appellation is of course Châteauneuf-du-Pape. There are many reasons why Châteauneuf-du-Pape is so famous, over and above the reputation of its wines. It was the first area to be delimited by the fledgling Appellation Contrôlée system in 1931. A staggering 13 different grape varieties are permitted under the rules. Some of the vineyards have an extraordinary 'pudding stones' (*galets* in French) soil. As well as providing good drainage and limiting vine vigour, the rocks heat up during the day and then at night act like a night storage heater. This extra help in ripening the grapes is part of the reason why Châteauneuf-du-Pape ends up with such brain-numbing alcohol levels. One of the village's weirder claims to fame is that it is illegal to land flying saucers (or for that matter flying cigars – should you own one) in the vineyards.

Although 13 grape varieties are permitted for Châteauneuf-du-Pape, the usual southern Rhône quartet (Grenache, Cinsault, Mourvèdre and Syrah) are the major players. In spite, or perhaps because, of its fame red Châteauneuf-du-Pape is very variable in both style and quality. The best advice to consumers is to taste before buying, and once you have found a producer whose wines you like, follow him rather than just buying any old Châteauneuf-du-Pape. There is a small amount of dry white Châteauneuf-du-Pape produced as well as the ubiquitous red. A wine that is grown, fermented, matured and bottled in the village of Châteauneuf-du-Pape is entitled to use a heavy glass bottle embossed with the papal insignia. This is a reminder of the period in the Middle Ages when the Popes resided just down the road from Châteauneuf-du-Pape in Avignon.

AC Gigondas, AC Vacqueyras and AC Lirac

These three appellations are all capable of producing impressive, full-bodied reds in the Châteauneuf-du-Pape mould. However, being less well known the prices can be competitive.

AC Tavel

Tavel is reckoned to be the best rosé in France. It is dry and has more weight and concentration than one normally associates with rosés.

AC Muscat de Beaumes de Venise

In Britain, Muscat de Beaumes de Venise has long been a stalwart of the dessert trolley. However, this fortified sweet white wine is actually delicious when drunk chilled as an apéritif. The Muscat gives the wine its floral and grapey aroma. Muscat de Beaumes de Venise is the most famous example of a whole family of fortified sweet wines produced in southern France and known as *vins doux naturels*.

AC Rasteau

This is a *vin doux naturel* made from the Grenache rather than the Muscat. It therefore usually comes out as a fortified sweet red wine.

AC Coteaux du Tricastin, AC Côtes du Ventoux and AC Côtes du Lubéron

These three areas are all satellites of the main southern Rhône vineyards. They are capable of producing some decent quaffing reds.

Pudding stones at Châteauneuf-du-Pape. How could anyone have thought of growing vines on such barren land?

The world of wine

Provence & Languedoc-Roussillon

Languedoc-Roussillon is France's great Table Wine factory. That said, through its varietal Vin de Pays wines, Languedoc is now giving the trendy countries of the New World a run for their money. Provence is best known for its uncomplicated, swig-on-the-beach, dry rosés. However, the inquisitive will also want to try some of the region's top reds.

PROVENCE

The Mediterranean climate of Provence allows the production of soft, open-hearted, immediately appealing wines. There are some more structured, 'serious' wines, but Provence's wines are primarily about youthful quaffability. The line-up of black grapes follows the pattern of the southern Rhône, with Grenache, Cinsault and Mourvèdre featuring prominently. The Midi's workhorse grape, the Carignan, is important, but a lot of Cabernet Sauvignon and Syrah have been planted over the last 20 years to beef up some of the reds.

Much of the region's famous rosé is sold in the curvaceous Provençal bottle. The dry whites from Provence are simple and light. Like the rosés they are best drunk in their first flush of youth when they are fresh and vibrant. Many of the reds are also designed for drinking young. However, as indicated above, there are a number of estates working at producing powerful, concentrated, age-worthy red wines that can stand comparison with their peers from elsewhere in France.

Most of Provence's vineyards are covered by three appellations; Coteaux d'Aix-en-Provence, Coteaux Varois and Côtes de Provence. Two small areas with their own appellations are Bandol and Bellet. AC Bandol lies just to the west of Toulon and is best known for its robust Mourvèdre-based reds. AC Bellet is near Nice and makes some surprisingly stylish, aromatic dry whites.

LANGUEDOC-ROUSSILLON

Stretching from the River Rhône to the Spanish border, Languedoc-Roussillon is the largest vineyard region in France. With around 350,000 ha (875,000 acres) under vine, the Midi (an alternative name for this region) is three times the size of Bordeaux, the next largest vineyard region in France. Although Languedoc-Roussillon enjoys a favourable Mediterranean climate with mild winters and warm summers, it is not immune from inclement weather. Spring frost, rain during the harvest period, and apocalyptic storms have all affected parts of the Midi over recent years.

From wine lake to Vin de Pays

The region has a venerable wine producing tradition going back to ancient times. Yet the Midi's modern role is one of bulk wine production. You have only to see the looks on tourists' faces when they see wine being dispensed by petrol pump into jerry cans to realise we are a long way from the Médoc or the Côte d'Or. Languedoc's position as France's commodity wine producer was

Côtes de Provence Rosé, Cave de Lorgues 2000

Very pale pink. Clean and simple on the nose. Light intensity. Youthful pear drop aromas. A hint of strawberry jam. Dry, lowish acidity, moderate alcohol. Light-bodied. A similar approachable fruitiness as on the nose. Short finish.

103

Sun-drenched Provence, home to the famous lavender fields and glugging rosés.

established during the second half of the nineteenth century. *Phylloxera* had devastated many of the vineyards around Paris that traditionally supplied the capital with its plonk; meanwhile, the opening of the railway from Languedoc to Paris meant that cheap wine produced in the south could be transported with ease to the thirsty masses of the north.

This trade in Vin de Table started to struggle in the years after the Second World War. France's per capita wine consumption began to slide at exactly the same time that the production side was becoming more efficient. The millions of litres of unwanted wine created the 'Wine Lake' of tabloid myth. A scheme was set up that paid growers to grub up their vineyards to try to tackle the over-production problem. At the same time the Vin de Pays category was created to give growers and consumers something to aspire to at the marketing end. These measures took their time to have any significant effect. However, the momentum towards improved quality has gradually built up, fuelled by investment from France and overseas. It is now not hyperbole to say that for many commentators Languedoc-Roussillon is the most exciting and innovative region in France.

There is still a sizeable production of Vin de Table. Grape varieties like Aramon and Carignan traditionally form the base of these hairy reds.

However, the future would definitely seem to be with Vin de Pays. The departmental Vins de Pays of Gard, Hérault, Aude and Pyrénées-Orientales are all in the Midi. Even more frequently seen though is the regional Vin de Pays d'Oc, which covers the whole of Languedoc-Roussillon.

Many producers have realised that it makes sense to focus on the well-known 'Vin de Pays d'Oc', rather than use one of the more obscure local Vin de Pays names (of which there are nearly 100). The option to use varietal labelling for Vin de Pays has been a crucial element in the success of these wines. Much as traditionalists and the Appellation Contrôlée authorities may regret it, we do live in a varietal age. If a grower is going to plant Chardonnay and Cabernet Sauvignon in Languedoc-Roussillon then they should be able to communicate that fact to the consumer. Other non-traditional varieties to have been planted in the region include Sauvignon Blanc, Chenin Blanc, Viognier, Merlot, Pinot Noir and Syrah. The whole armoury of modern winemaking (pneumatic presses, stainless steel vats, refrigeration, sterile filtration etc.) has been deployed to make the most of these classic grape varieties.

While the Table Wine vineyards of the plain have been undergoing their well-publicised metamorphosis, big improvements have been taking place in the hills. There is now a string of appellations that runs from outside Nîmes to the Spanish border: AC Costières de Nîmes; AC Coteaux du Languedoc; AC Faugères; AC St-Chinian; AC Minervois; AC Corbières; AC Fitou; AC Côtes du Roussillon. The worst examples of these wines are indistinguishable from Vin de Table. However, the better estates and co-operatives are making attractive wines at sensible prices. The best examples are reds, with Carignan and the southern Rhône black grapes making up the blend. The dry whites and rosés produced by some of these appellations are simple wines for drinking young.

Far left: If you think this vineyard looks beautiful, wait until you see the one over the page!

Vins doux naturels

As well as the huge volume of light wine produced in the Midi, the region is responsible for a number of fortified sweet wines (*vins doux naturels*). Those based on Muscat are: AC Muscat de Lunel; AC Muscat de Mireval; AC Muscat de Frontignan; AC Muscat de St-Jean-de-Minervois; AC Muscat de Rivesaltes. Those based on Grenache, Muscat and other grapes are: AC Banyuls; AC Maury; AC Rivesaltes. The red version of Banyuls can be rich and impressive. It is the nearest thing in France to Port. A version called 'Banyuls Rancio' is produced by maturing the wine in barrels out of doors. The summer heat causes the wine to develop an almost Madeira-like character.

Sparkling wines

Tucked a little way inland from the Corbières vineyards is the town of Limoux. It has long been famous for the production of sparkling wines. Most are made by the traditional method. AC Blanquette de Limoux is the designation for wines based primarily on the local Mauzac grape. AC Crémant de Limoux covers the wines based on Chardonnay and Chenin Blanc.

CORSICA

Corsica used to be famous as a source of cheap bulk wines. Whilst in many cases the quality is still fairly basic, there are some better wines being produced nowadays. The whole island is covered by the Vin de Pays de l'Ile de Beauté and the AC Vin de Corse.

THE SOUTH-WEST

Between Languedoc-Roussillon and Bordeaux there are a scattering of vineyard areas that are still relatively poorly known outside France. Part of the reason is that although they are lumped together under 'south-western France', many of them are quite distinctive. This is because of differences of climate, *terroir* and grape variety. On the latter point, the South-West has its own very distinctive repertoire of grapes, some of which (Malbec and Tannat) are becoming better known.

A Provençal vineyard overlooking the Mediterranean Sea (stop fantasising about buying a vineyard right now).

AC Gaillac

The appellation covers just about all wine styles known to man (red, rosé, dry white, sweet white, sparkling). They are often pleasant but never profound. Local grape varieties such as Duras, Fer and Len de l'El are usually backed up by some of the Bordeaux regulars (Cabernet Sauvignon, Cabernet Franc, Merlot, Sauvignon Blanc and Sémillon). On the export markets a lot of white wine from the Gaillac area sells as Vin de Pays du Tarn, rather than using the appellation.

AC Côtes du Frontonnais

These are fruity, gluggable reds and rosés made principally from the local Negrette grape (with varieties like Cabernet Sauvignon and Gamay making up the blend).

AC Cahors

Cahors at its best is a robust and chunky red wine. The key grape is the Malbec. It will be interesting to see if the increasing identification of this variety with Argentina will benefit or disadvantage Cahors in markets like the UK.

AC Côtes de Duras

This Bordeaux satellite is best known for the production of dry white wines based on Sauvignon Blanc and Sémillon.

AC Buzet

Another Bordeaux satellite, but here it is the area's red wines that merit mention. As you would expect, Merlot, Cabernet Sauvignon and also Cabernet Franc are the principal grape varieties employed.

Vin de Pays des Côtes de Gascogne

With the decline in Armagnac distillation a number of producers have focused on making decent dry white wines that can sell in their own right. The grape varieties are those traditionally used to make Armagnac, Ugni Blanc and Colombard. These wines tend to sell as Vin de Pays des Côtes de Gascogne or Vin de Pays de Gers.

VDQS Côtes de St-Mont

Not a bad source of inexpensive reds, rosés and dry whites. It is mainly local grapes that are used, with the Tannat the leading black variety.

AC Madiran

This would be many pundits' nomination as the South-West's top red wine appellation. Based on the Tannat, with contributions from Cabernet Franc, Cabernet Sauvignon and Fer, Madiran can be tough and unforgiving when young. With bottle age the rough edges are smoothed out and a complex bouquet develops.

AC Pacherenc du Vic-Bilh

This can be an attractive sweet white wine made from a blend of white grapes including the Petit Manseng and the Gros Manseng.

AC Jurançon

Jurançon is the South-West's finest white wine. The sweet version is traditionally made from late harvested Petit Manseng, which may or may not have succumbed to Noble Rot. The Jurançon Sec is normally produced from the Gros Manseng.

Whilst the Middle East can lay claim to being the cradle of viticulture, it is Europe that has been the main centre of wine production for the last 2000 years. The vine, the olive tree and corn have formed the basis of Mediterranean agriculture since classical times, and even nowadays Europe accounts for something like three-quarters of the world's wine production.

However, Europe's wine producers have had to face up to some monumental changes in the second half of the twentieth century. Wine consumption in most parts of southern Europe has fallen

Europe

sharply. Not only are people drinking less, they are drinking better quality wine. The market for the traditional peasant 'rot gut' is slowly trickling away.

The structure of the wine industry in many parts of Europe is also hopelessly outdated. Based on fragmented land-holdings and manual vineyard work, the introduction of mechanisation and also high employment costs have re-written the economics of contemporary viticulture. In addition, ever-increasing competition from the New World has focused the attention of politicians and bureaucrats, as well as people in the wine industry, on the need for rapid change.

Where wine producers have aimed for efficiency and quality there have been some great successes. There is absolutely no reason why Europe's wine producers should not produce wines with the same technical competence as the New World competition, while at the same time respecting the best traditions of their own native regions.

As wine consumers, we should respond by being adventurous and open minded when we select our wines.

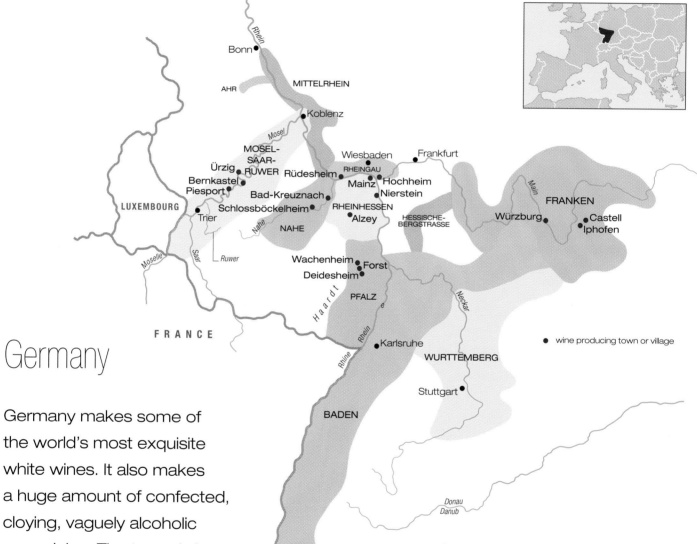

Bonn

AHR

MITTELRHEIN

Koblenz

Mosel

MOSEL-
SAAR-
RUWER

Ürzig

Bernkastel

Rüdesheim

Wiesbaden

Frankfurt

RHEINGAU

Hochheim

Mainz

Nierstein

Piesport

Bad-Kreuznach

LUXEMBOURG

Schlossböckelheim

RHEINHESSEN

Alzey

Trier

Nahe

NAHE

HESSISCHE-
BERGSTRASSE

FRANKEN

Würzburg

Castell

Iphofen

Main

Moselle

Saar

Ruwer

Wachenheim

Forst

Deidesheim

Haardt

PFALZ

Neckar

FRANCE

Rhine

Karlsruhe

WURTTEMBERG

Rhein

Stuttgart

BADEN

Donau
Danub

wine producing town or village

BADEN

WURTTEMBERG

Basel

Bodensee

SWITZERLAND

The world of wine

Germany

Germany makes some of
the world's most exquisite
white wines. It also makes
a huge amount of confected,
cloying, vaguely alcoholic
grape juice. The tragedy is
that in key export markets
like the UK the average
punter thinks that all German
wines are like the latter rather
than the former.

Fine German wines have long been appreciated in Britain. What distorted our appreciation of German wines was the boom in Liebfraumilch sales in the 1980s. With sales figures through the roof, it was hard to argue with the wine trade that all was not for the best. The problem was that all German wine was coming to be thought of as cheap, inconsequential swill. When in the 1990s consumers started to trade up (and tastes became drier), German wines were left standing. No amount of re-packaging and re-launching can get over the fact that most wine drinkers think German wines are naff. We may well have to wait for a younger generation of wine drinkers to come through who are untainted by Liebfraumilch and can objectively appreciate the quality of Germany's finest wines.

With almost exactly 100,000 ha (250,000 acres) of vineyard, Germany is by no means a large wine producer. Bordeaux alone has 117,000 ha (292,500 acres) under vine. What is more, most of Germany's wine regions are clustered in the south-western corner of the country, near to the River Rhein or one of its tributaries.

Cool climate and delicate wines

The 50th degree of latitude runs through the Rheingau, Germany's most famous vineyard region. This means that Germany has the coolest climate of any of the world's major wine producing countries. Consequently it is best known for its production of delicately fruity white wines, which are high in acidity and low in alcohol. For the home market in Germany many of these wines are vinified dry, and sold with the label description *Trocken* (dry) or *Halbtrocken* (off-dry). For most export markets the wines are made in a medium style. This can be achieved by stopping the fermentation before all the sugar has been used up, or by the addition of *süssreserve* (*see page 61*). Certainly in the coolest regions of Germany, like the Mosel-Saar-Ruwer, a little residual sweetness is necessary to balance off the very high natural acidity.

Wine drinkers outside Germany are often surprised to discover that the country actually makes red wine. In fact something like 15% of the national production is red wine. German red wines are usually light and delicate in style, and in many cases little more than glorified rosés.

The Germans are the biggest consumers of sparkling wine in the world. The fizz produced in Germany itself is called Sekt. Most of it is made by the tank method.

German grape varieties

Riesling This is the great aristocrat amongst the German grape varieties. Even when fully ripe the Riesling grape maintains an excellent backbone of acidity. This helps to give the sweeter wines great balance, and also allows them to age gracefully. The rub with Riesling is that it ripens very late. In the Mosel Valley the Riesling harvest does not usually get under way until October and may run on into November. This is obviously something of a gamble given that the weather may have deteriorated by then. One way to improve the chances of getting the Riesling grape ripe is to plant the vines on the best, steep, well-drained vineyard sites.

**Kendermann Mosel
Riesling Spätlese 2000**

Pale greenish lemon. Soft, gentle, green fruit on the nose. Pear and quince. Slightly floral. Medium dry, very high acidity, light alcohol. Light-bodied, but with a decent backbone of fruit. Shortish finish.

Silvaner Apart from a few devotees, Silvaner is pretty much unloved nowadays. Without the class of Riesling, Silvaner's big selling point is that it ripens earlier than Riesling. The fruit character of Silvaner is rather flat and neutral.

Müller-Thurgau (Rivaner) Müller-Thurgau is a cross that was developed at the end of the nineteenth century. This grape variety ripens very early and produces a big crop. For these reasons it became hugely popular in the last century, for a considerable period overtaking Riesling in terms of vineyard acreage. Where Müller-Thurgau falls down is that it lacks the elegance of Riesling, some people also disliking its floral aroma.

Scheurebe Of all the crosses based on Riesling, Scheurebe has attracted the most praise from quality-conscious grape growers. The best examples have a lovely, pure, almost grapefruit-like aroma.

Rülander (Grauburgunder) This is none other than the Pinot Gris. Like its brother in Alsace, it produces wines with good fruit and some weight on the palate.

Spätburgunder This is another French variety in disguise, as Spätburgunder is Pinot Noir. The Spätburgunder produces the lightest of light red wines. When young they can show the scented red fruit character associated with Pinot Noir.

The majestic sweep of the River Mosel near Trittenheim.

Dornfelder This relatively recent cross has created quite a lot of interest. Dornfelder is a black variety of grape, which even in Germany is capable of producing darkly coloured red wines. There is sometimes a touch of brambley fruit. The palate structure is relatively light though.

German wine law

Although the Germans use the same Table Wine / Quality Wine framework as the French, the basis for a wine's rating is totally different. For the French, it is a wine's origin, and in particular its *terroir*, that determines the quality status. In Burgundy, for example, whether a wine is a Grand Cru or a Premier Cru depends on which field it

came from. By contrast, the Germans focus less on *terroir* and more on how ripe the grapes are when they are picked. The higher the sugar level in the grapes at harvest time, the further up the quality scale the wine will go. The scale of sweetness used in Germany is 'Oechsle', and it is a must's Oechsle reading that determines where in the hierarchy the wine will end up.

Tafelwein

This is something of a red herring as very often it is not German wine at all. Although the bottle and label may look very Teutonic, the contents will probably be a 'Euro-blend'. There is nothing illegal about producing a blended Table Wine with the liquid drawn from one or more European Union (EU) countries. However, Tafelwein now has to state clearly, in the language of the country in which it is being sold, that it is a blend of wines from several countries in the EU.

Deutscher Tafelwein

Deutscher Tafelwein is the basic German Table Wine and therefore will have been made from the least ripe grapes. It is equivalent to France's Vin de Table. Mosel Deutscher Tafelwein and Hock Deutscher Tafelwein are the two main versions seen on the export markets. Hock is the nickname in the English-speaking world for wines from vineyards along the River Rhein.

Deutscher Landwein

This is Germany's version of Vin de Pays. The grapes have to reach a slightly higher ripeness level than those used for Deutscher Tafelwein. The rules for Deutscher Landwein state that it has to be produced either in a *Trocken* (dry) or a *Halbtrocken* (off-dry) style. This requirement has

The world of wine

hindered the development of Deutscher Landwein sales in markets that expect their German wines to be medium sweet.

Qualitätswein bestimmter Anbaugebiete (QbA)

Qualitätswein bestimmter Anbaugebiete can be translated as 'quality wine from a designated region'. Mercifully this category is invariably referred to as 'Qualitätswein' or just 'QbA'. Being the German system the grapes will have more sugar than those used for the Table Wines. However, it is still necessary to chaptalise QbA wines to get the required final alcohol level. QbA is equivalent to VDQS in the French hierarchy. There are 13 Anbaugebiete (wine regions) in Germany. All German quality wines will tell you on the label which one they are from. A further aspect of the German wine law insists that each batch of quality wine has to be analysed and tasted before being issued with a government control number (the 'Amtliche Prüfungsnummer' or 'AP Number'). This number then has to appear on the label of every bottle of wine in the batch. Although bureaucratic, it does mean that if there is ever a query about the actual contents of one of these bottles, a check can be made against the original analysis. Commercially, QbA is extremely important as it is the legal status accorded to wines such as Liebfraumilch, Piesporter Michelsberg and Niersteiner Gutes Domtal.

Qualitätswein mit Prädikat (QmP)

This is the highest grade of wine in Germany and is therefore the German equivalent of Appellation Contrôlée. The ripest grapes go into QmP, with no chaptalisation allowed. The same system of Anbaugebiete and AP Numbers applies to QmP as to QbA. The QmP category is sub-divided based on just exactly how much sugar there is in the grapes at harvest. Weather permitting, you can think of these categories as representing harvest date. The longer the grapes stay on the vine, the more sugar they will accumulate, the further up the scale the resulting wine will go. Inevitably, given the vagaries of the German autumn, the further up the scale you go the smaller the volumes will be and the higher the prices.

Eiswein When grapes have been left on the vine in the hope of getting Noble Rot but little or no *Botrytis* infection has occurred, all is not quite lost. The growers will leave these grapes on the vine right through until the middle of the winter. When the first severe frost occurs, -8°C (18°F) or lower, usually in December or January, the frozen grapes are picked. By pressing these grapes whilst still

QmP categories

Kabinett
These grapes will be picked a little later than those for QbA. German Kabinett wines are amongst the world's most delicate white wines.

Spätlese
Spätlese literally means late gathered. When made from Riesling, these can be the purest expression of that grape.

Auslese
At this level the wines are usually getting decidedly sweet.

Beerenauslese
This sweet wine is made in fine autumns when there is Noble Rot (*Edelfäule*).

Trockenbeerenauslese
This is the greatest, sweetest and rarest category of German wine. It is possible to make Trockenbeerenauslese only when Noble Rot has reduced the grapes to desiccated raisins.

frozen a very sweet juice is released. This is used to make the third of Germany's great sweet wines, Eiswein. In terms of Oechsle reading, Eiswein grapes have to contain at least as much sugar as Beerenauslese grapes.

Wine names

One of the main difficulties in trying to sell better-quality German wines are the intimidating labels that confront the consumer. Apart from an irrational terror of the German language, particularly when written in Gothic script, many of the labels go in for information overload. Even after identifying the quality status, grape variety and region, the punter still has to wrestle with the wine's actual origin. However, like most issues relating to wine the world over, once you have mastered a few basic rules German labels are not scary at all.

Einzellagen and Grosslagen

Many German wines have double-barrelled names, such as Wehlener Sonnenuhr. The first word (usually ending in '-er', meaning 'from') is the name of the village where the wine originates. In the current example, the village is Wehlen. The second word is the name of the vineyard (in this case, Sonnenuhr). The one complication comes over the actual size of the vineyard. The German word for a single vineyard is an *Einzellage*. Most of Germany's finest wines will come from individual sites like this (Sonnenuhr is an Einzellage).

As well as these Einzellagen, there are much larger entities called *Grosslagen*. Instead of referring to one field, a Grosslage will usually cover dozens of vineyards spread across a number of villages. The 'Michelsberg' of Piesporter Michelsberg and the 'Gutes Domtal' of Niersteiner Gutes Domtal are Grosslagen. One of the weaknesses of this system is that the wine label does not tell you whether a vineyard name is an Einzellage or a Grosslage. So unless you are a German wine expert, or you have easy access to a book on German wine, you do not know whether you are buying a wine from a field the size of a football pitch, or a wine that is a blend from dozens of fields that are scattered across several villages.

Bereiche

A *Bereich* is a wine growing district, sometimes covering the same area as an English county. For instance, the enormous Pfalz region is divided into two Bereiche, Mittelhaardt-Deutsche Weinstrasse and Südliche Weinstrasse. Not surprisingly, these Bereich wines will tend to be inexpensive blends put together by large merchants or co-operative cellars. The two most frequently seen in the UK are Bereich Nierstein and Bereich Bernkastel. Amidst all the blurb on a label, two other words are worth looking out for:

Erzeugerabfüllung This indicates that the wine was bottled by its producer. It is not as exclusive as it sounds because the producer may be a co-operative winery.

Gutsabfüllung This is a stricter endorsement as it indicates that a wine was actually grown, fermented, matured and bottled on the estate. It is equivalent to 'Mis en bouteille au château/domaine' on a French wine label.

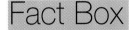

Fact Box

Liebfraumilch

The widest drawn category of German wine is Liebfraumilch, with its own set of rules:

It has to be a fruity, medium white wine.

It can be only of QbA quality.

It has to come from one of the following Anbaugebiete: Rheinhessen (the most important one), Pfalz, Rheingau and Nahe.

A blend of traditional German grapes is used (usually mainly Müller-Thurgau and Silvaner).

No details of grape variety or vineyard are allowed on the label.

Wine regions (Anbaugebiete)
Mosel-Saar-Ruwer

This region takes its name from the River Mosel and its two vine growing tributaries, the Saar and the Ruwer. Lying to the north-west of most of the other German vineyards, the Mosel-Saar-Ruwer

Piesport, the tiny Mosel village that gives its name to Piesporter Michelsberg.

The world of wine

has a particularly cool climate. As a result of this the wines are crisp and steely. The best wines are produced from Riesling vines planted on the steep slate slopes above the rivers. These wines have a finesse and delicacy found nowhere else in the world. The flatter, less favourable sites are planted with Müller-Thurgau. Famous wine villages in the region include Piesport, Bernkastel, Wehlen and Ürzig. Traditionally most of the wines from the Mosel-Saar-Ruwer are bottled in green flute bottles.

Nahe

The Nahe wines are generally thought of as being intermediate in style between the wines of the Mosel and those of the Rhein. The region's most famous vineyards have a sandstone soil and this is where the finest Rieslings are grown. As in the Mosel, the simpler wines are often made from Müller-Thurgau. Famous wine villages in the Nahe include Bad Kreuznach and Schlossböckelheim. Nahe wines, along with those from the main Rhein regions, are traditionally bottled in brown flute bottles.

Rheingau

Although in volume terms the Rheingau is a small region, it is generally reckoned to produce the finest wines in Germany. Riesling is the dominant grape. Most of the vineyards are located on the sheltered south-facing slope immediately overlooking the River Rhein. As far as Riesling is concerned, the conditions are nigh on perfect for achieving ripeness without sacrificing elegance. The roster of wine producing villages includes

Rüdesheim, Johannisberg, Hattenheim, Eltville, Kiedrich and Hochheim. It was the name of the latter village that got shortened to 'Hock', a slang term now applied to all Rhein wines. The village of Geisenheim is the location of the famous German wine research centre. As well as great sweet wines, the Rheingau does make some impressive dry Rieslings. You might want to look out for wines approved under the 'Charta' scheme.

Rheinhessen

The Rheinhessen, and its neighbour to the south, the Pfalz, are the two mega-volume regions of Germany. Most of the Rheinhessen's production is simple wine. This, after all, is where a great deal of the Liebfraumilch comes from. Whilst there are some fine sloping vineyards overlooking the Rhein, much of the Rheinhessen's production comes from high-yielding vineyards on relatively flat land. Müller-Thurgau and Silvaner are the principal grape varieties. Nierstein, Oppenheim and Alzey are three important wine producing villages.

Pfalz (also known as the Rheinpfalz or the Palatinate)

The Pfalz lies directly to the south of the Rheinhessen. It has a dry climate due to the sheltering effect of the Haardt mountains (in effect the northern extension of the Vosges mountains that shelter the Alsace region). Within the Pfalz's large total production there is a big variation in quality. Like the Rheinhessen, a significant chunk of the wine is basic stuff made from the Müller-Thurgau. However, there are some fine Rieslings.

The Scheurebe and Gewürztraminer are also responsible for some interesting wines. Top villages include Wachenheim, Forst, Deidesheim and Bad Dürkheim.

Baden

Baden enjoys the warmest climate of any of Germany's wine producing regions. This means that the grapes will often be relatively high in sugar and low in acidity. The resulting wines are usually quite high in alcohol by German standards, and with soft acidity there is no need to sweeten them up. Hence, most of the white wines in Baden are sold bone dry. The key white grape varieties are Müller-Thurgau and Grauburgunder. The warmth of Baden also favours red wine production. In fact, Spätburgunder is the region's most widely planted grape variety. Many of Baden's finest wines come from vineyards planted on the slopes of an extinct volcano called the Kaiserstuhl.

Franken

This region lies along the River Main, with the beautiful city of Würzburg at its heart. Like Baden, most of the wines are vinified dry. Some of Germany's finest Silvaners come from Franken. Castell and Iphofen are two famous wine producing villages. Franken traditionally uses a flask-shaped bottle called a 'bocksbeutel' for its wines.

The following six Anbaugebiete rarely export their wines: Ahr, Mittelrhein, Hessische Bergstrasse, Württemberg, Saale-Unstrut and Sachsen. The last two are located in the former East Germany.

The world of wine

Italy

Italy is the world's largest wine producer. That in itself makes the subject of Italian wine potentially intimidating. Italian wine law adds to the fun by defining an enormous number of wine producing areas, many of which are barely known to your average Master of Wine, never mind to a normal wine drinker in her local 'trat'.

Even once you have got your head around Barbera and Barbaresco, Montepulciano d'Abruzzo and Vino Nobile di Montepulciano, there comes one final layer of bewildering complexity. Italy, when it comes to premium wine production, is a nation of individualists. In striving for quality, today's top growers don't care what their father or grandfather did, or what some rule says you can or can't do. What is more, they are often producing wine in such tiny quantities that getting hold of a few bottles becomes a fanatical pursuit in itself. Nevertheless, these enormously characterful wines are worth searching out, not least because they offer a counterbalance to the vast volumes of dull, neutral plonk that still come out of Italy.

Italian wine law

The structure and administration of the wine law has been the cause of much controversy and revision in the past. At its simplest, it is modelled on the French hierarchy.

Vino da Tavola

This is Italy's basic table wine.

Indicazione Geografica Tipica (IGT)

IGT is Italy's answer to Vin de Pays. These wines are now available on export markets.

Denominazione di Origine Controllata (DOC)

The lower level of quality wine in Italy is DOC. Many of Italy's most famous wines are covered by DOC. Gradually the best of the DOCs are being promoted up to DOCG.

Denominazione di Origine Controllata e Garantita (DOCG)

This is the highest grade of Italian wine.

The wine regions of Italy

Italy enjoys the quintessential Mediterranean climate (mild, wet winters; warm, dry summers). However, from a wine perspective, there is a huge climatic variation between the north and south. Torino lies further north than Bordeaux, while Marsala (at the western end of Sicily) is a mere 150 km (94 miles) from Tunisia. Altitude has a big effect on the climate, with the location of vineyards varying from sea level up to 1000 m (3280 ft).

Additional label endorsements

Classico
The wine has come from vineyards in the historic centre of a district.

Secco means dry.
Dolce means sweet.
Abbocato or **Amabile** means medium sweet.

Riserva
The wine has received extended maturation in wood and/or bottle.

Annata indicates year.
Vendemmia indicates vintage.
Vecchio means old.

Superiore
The wine has achieved a higher minimum alcohol level than that specified for the basic DOC or DOCG. This designation is being phased out.

Azienda Agricola is a wine estate.
Cantina Sociale is a co-operative winery.

Consorzio
Most DOC and DOCG districts have an association of producers called a Consorzio. The most famous of these is the Chianti Classico Consorzio (the black cockerel neck label indicates that a grower is a member).

119

Italy

The world of wine

PIEMONTE

Piemonte in volume terms is not a large region. However, many would say that this coolish region produces some of Italy's finest red wines.

A short distance south-east of Torino is the town of Alba, and it is in the surrounding Langhe hills that the great red wines are produced. DOCG Barolo and DOCG Barbaresco are strongly flavoured, savoury red wines made from the Nebbiolo grape. With the grainy tannins and tarry fruit of this variety, young Barolo can be intimidating. However, with bottle age it becomes more mellow. As well as Nebbiolo, the area around Alba and Asti also grows two other quality black grapes, the Barbera and the Dolcetto. The Barbera produces elegant mid-bodied reds (e.g. DOC Barbera d'Asti). The wines made from Dolcetto are fruity, with a soft lushness on the palate (e.g. DOC Dolcetto d'Alba).

North-east of Torino, DOCG Gattinara is a robust red made from Nebbiolo, usually tempered by the addition of another black grape called Bonarda. Nebbiolo is sometimes sold under its alternative names, Spanna and Chiavennasca.

Vineyards high up in Trentino-Alto Adige (the same heart-lifting view that confronted Goethe when he crossed the Brenner Pass).

The most famous white wine produced in Piemonte is DOCG Asti. This medium sweet sparkling wine is made by a variation on the tank method. The Moscato (Muscat) grape is responsible for the wine's perfumed, grapey aroma. DOCG Moscato d'Asti is a slightly more elegant and less fizzy version of Asti. The fashionable DOCG Gavi is also from Piemonte. This neutral dry white wine is made from the Cortese grape.

The regions of Liguria and Valle d'Aosta are small wine producers that export very little.

LOMBARDIA

Centred on Milano, Lombardia is Italy's industrial and commercial powerhouse, and wine production is not a big priority. However, there are some interesting niches of viticulture. In the Alpine valley of the River Adda is DOCG Valtellina Superiore. This mid- to full-bodied red wine is made from the Nebbiolo grape. DOCG Franciacorta is reckoned by many to be Italy's finest traditional method sparkling wine. The still wines (red and white) from the same area sell as DOC Terre di Franciacorta. A mixture of Italian (Barbera, Nebbiolo) and French (Cabernet Sauvignon, Chardonnay) grape varieties are grown. DOC Oltrepò Pavese can be red, rosé, white or sparkling, and made from grapes as diverse as Moscato and Pinot Noir. Over on the western shore of Lake Garda is DOC Lugana, a dry white wine made from the Trebbiano grape.

TRENTINO-ALTO ADIGE

This spectacular, mountainous region stretches from just north of Verona all the way up to the Brenner Pass. Politically the region was part of Austria until the end of the First World War. As you travel up the Adige Valley the predominant language changes from Italian to German. For this reason the wines from the top end of the valley are sometimes labelled as 'Südtiroler' (from the South Tyrol) rather than 'Alto Adige'.

With its cool climate, it is not surprising that the region is best known in Britain for its dry white wines. These are often made from grape varieties like Chardonnay, Pinot Grigio, Pinot Bianco and Riesling. The wines tend to be light and crisp interpretations of these varieties. Some mid-bodied reds from Cabernet Sauvignon and Merlot are also made. Most of these wines sell as either DOC Trentino or DOC Alto Adige / Südtiroler. The DOC Santa Maddalena covers a mid-bodied red made from a local grape called the Schiava.

VENETO

The Veneto is a large wine producing region. While much of its wine is dull, there are some interesting speciality wines, as well as some individual growers whose efforts are noteworthy.

Clustered around Verona are the region's three most famous wines: DOC Soave, DOC Valpolicella and DOC Bardolino. Soave is a light, neutral dry white wine made from Garganega and Trebbiano. Using just Garganega grapes from vineyards on the hills around the town of Soave, a more characterful dry white can be produced. Valpolicella and Bardolino are light-bodied red wines made from a blend of local black grapes, the most important of which is the Corvina.

Although most Valpolicella is nothing to write home about, there are some versions that are

Best Buy

Barolo, Terre del Barolo 1996

Mid-pale brick red core. Broad terracotta rim. A broad and savoury bouquet develops in the glass. Figs, dates and prunes. Verging on leathery and vegetal. Dry, mid-acidity, high alcohol. Fairly full-bodied. Chewy, austere, astringent tannins come through on the palate. Ink and liquorice. Mid-length. This example is drinking well and will hold for a few more years.

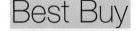

Best Buy

Pinot Grigio, Trentino, Mezzacorona 2000

Very pale lemon. Clean and light. The fruit character is very delicate. Touches of pear and banana. Dry, mid-acidity, moderate alcohol. Very light-bodied. There is a simple green fruit character in the mouth. Short, crisp finish.

more than worthy of note. There is a tradition in many parts of Italy of making wines from grapes that have been dried indoors. Such wines are often referred to as 'passito' wines. Two wines are made in the Valpolicella area from Corvina grapes that have been dried on wooden racks. 'Amarone della Valpolicella' is a powerful, astringent dry red wine. In this case, after drying and crushing, the yeast were able to ferment out all the sugar present in the grapes. The resulting wine will have a heroic alcohol level, sometimes as high as 16%ABV. Recioto della Valpolicella is made the same way, except the yeast conk out leaving the wine sweet. The third upmarket Valpolicella variant uses the lees left in the barrels or vats after the Recioto has been racked. With a 'ripasso' wine normal Valpolicella is run into the vessel containing the Recioto lees. Because the latter still contains sugar and yeast, a second burst of fermentation is stimulated. Valpolicella made this way is fuller and rounder than a standard version.

A small amount of sweet Soave, Recioto di Soave, is made from dried white grapes. This version of Soave has been granted its own DOCG.

Other DOCs in the Veneto include Lison-Pramaggiore (some decent reds) and Prosecco di Conegliano-Valdobbiadene (cheapish fizz).

FRIULI-VENEZIA-GIULIA

Tucked up in the north-eastern corner of Italy, Friuli-Venezia-Giulia produces a vast line-up of varietal wines. The permitted varieties include:

White Chardonnay, Pinot Bianco, Pinot Grigio, Riesling, Sauvignon Blanc, Tocai Friulano, Gewürztraminer, Verduzzo and Picolit.

Black Cabernet Sauvignon, Cabernet Franc, Merlot, Pinot Nero and Refosco.

The general standard of winemaking is good, so even the basic wines are rarely disappointing. At the top end, the region is responsible for some impressive wines. The DOC Friuli-Grave accounts for a large proportion of the region's production. Smaller high-quality DOCs include Collio and Colli Orientali del Friuli.

EMILIA-ROMAGNA

Emilia-Romagna is infamous for the production of Lambrusco. Lambrusco is the name of the black grape used to make the wine. The Lambrusco seen on the export markets is medium sweet and semi-sparkling. It exists in red (rosso), rosé (rosato) and white (bianco) versions. At around 8%ABV, most of these wines are classified as Vino da Tavola. However, for markets like the UK, some producers will produce a version that is only 3%ABV. This stuff technically is not even wine (the labels often state 'Partially Fermented Grape Must'). The dry, semi-sparkling 'original' red Lambrusco is still produced, and some examples have DOC status.

The rather ordinary DOCG Albana di Romagna was the first white wine to be given DOCG status. Huge volumes of neutral dry white DOC Trebbiano di Romagna and lightish red DOC Sangiovese di Romagna are exported from the region.

MARCHE

The one really famous wine from this region is DOC Verdicchio dei Castelli di Jesi. This is a fresh, neutral dry white wine made from the

Best Buy

Chianti Classico Riserva, Vigna del Sorbo, Fontodi 1998

Deepish ruby core. Mid ruby-pink rim. Quite restrained on the nose at first. Then some dark fruit aromas come through. Plum and damson. Dry, lowish acidity and high alcohol. Mid-bodied. Some chewy astringent tannins are present. There is also a touch of cherrystone on the palate. Mid-long finish. Will keep well for around five years.

Verdicchio grape. DOC Rosso Conero (using the Montepulciano grape variety) and DOC Rosso Piceno (Montepulciano and Sangiovese) are decent, mid-bodied reds.

ABRUZZO

The Abruzzo has become famous as a source of moderately priced, mid-bodied reds made from the Montepulciano grape. They sell as DOC Montepulciano d'Abruzzo. The Molise region to the south also grows some Montepulciano.

TOSCANA

Nowhere is more evocative of Italy than Tuscany. A fundamental part of that magical landscape is the vine. Most famously, in the hills around Firenze and Siena are the vineyards that produce DOCG Chianti. Given the enormous volume that is produced, it is very hard to generalise about Chianti. It can vary from thin and wishy-washy to rich and concentrated, with a concomitant variation in price. Sangiovese forms the backbone of the Chianti blend, with contributions from a black

A landscape fit for Virgil.

Vineyards in Tuscany.

grape called Canaiolo and the white grapes Trebbiano and Malvasia. A small amount of Cabernet Sauvignon is now allowed in the blend as well. The first step in trying to track down serious Chianti is to focus on the wines produced in the historic centre of the region. The DOCG Chianti Classico covers this heartland, which lies directly in between Firenze and Siena. DOCG Chianti Rufina is another good sub-district worth looking out for.

DOCG Carmignano is a tiny area lying just west of Firenze. It is famous for its red wines based on Sangiovese / Cabernet Sauvignon blends. South of the Chianti region lie two fine

Sangiovese wines, DOCG Brunello di Montalcino and DOCG Vino Nobile di Montepulciano. Brunello in particular can be very dense and tannic when young.

Super Tuscans

The use of Cabernet Sauvignon in Tuscany has long been a controversial subject. Although there have been small plantings of Cabernet in Tuscany for centuries, when the DOC and DOCG rules were framed it was not a permitted variety for wines like Chianti. However, since the Second World War, many leading growers in Tuscany have experimented with Cabernet Sauvignon, and have succeeded in making some very fine wines. Perhaps the two most famous examples are 'Sassicaia' and 'Solaia'. The nickname given to these super-premium Cabernet-based wines was the 'Super Tuscans'. The great farce was that these wines, despite selling for ten times the price of bog standard Chianti, were classified only as Vino da Tavola. Very late in the day, the authorities are amending the DOC and DOCG rules to accommodate the Super Tuscans. The whole saga illustrates how badly wine legislation can reflect the actual quality of wine being made.

Tuscany's most highly regarded dry white wine is DOCG Vernaccia di San Gimignano. However, the region's one truly great white wine is Vin Santo. This is another of Italy's passito wines. Varying from medium through to lusciously sweet, and from light and youthful through to dark and oxidised, Vin Santo is one of Italy's vinous gems. It will come as no surprise to discover that most Vin Santo is sold as Vino da Tavola.

In the South. The odd, conical farm buildings, *trulle*, stand next to this vineyard in Puglia.

UMBRIA

This beautiful region is well known as the origin of DOC Orvieto. Most Orvieto nowadays is a dry white wine, although medium and sweet versions do exist. The grape varieties used include Trebbiano, Malvasia and Grechetto. DOCG Torgiano Reserva is a very serious red based on Sangiovese. The rich, sweet, passito red wine, DOCG Sagrantino di Montefalco is well worth seeking out as well.

LAZIO

The DOC Frascati vineyards lie in the hills just outside Roma. This immensely popular but generally quite neutral dry white wine is made from a blend of Malvasia and Trebbiano. Despite the exotic name, DOC Est! Est!! Est!!! di Montefiascone is the same sort of neutral white wine.

THE SOUTH

In the past most of the wine from southern Italy was written off as basic plonk. All that could be expected was for the wine to end up in a cheap Vino da Tavola blend, or to be tankered up to Torino for use in making Vermouth.

The region of Puglia has perhaps been the most successful in upgrading the quality of its wines. As well as attention to detail in the winery, the region has discovered that with some care several of its native black grapes can produce interesting wines. The varieties to look out for include Negroamaro, Malvasia Nera and Primitivo (which may be Zinfandel, *see page 48*). DOCs that are seen on the export market are Salice Salentino, Copertino and Primitivo di Manduria.

The one claim to fame of the Basilicata region is the full-bodied red, DOC Aglianico del Vulture. Calabria is not a big producer either, with Cirò being its most famous DOC (reds, rosés and dry whites). The Campania was renowned for its wine in Roman times (perhaps the most famous was 'Falernian'). Whilst most of the wine produced there today is pretty simple, DOCG Taurasi is a serious red based on the Aglianico grape.

SICILIA

Like the southern part of the mainland, much of the island's production is simple, everyday wine. Sicily's one world-famous wine is DOC Marsala. This fortified wine is produced at the western end of the island. Local white grapes, such as Grillo, are used to make a normal dry white wine. This is then fortified with grape spirit, and in most cases sweetened. The sweetening agents used include boiled-down grape must and grape must that has been prevented from fermenting through the addition of grape spirit (*mistela*). The Marsala is then matured, in some cases using a variation of the solera system (*see Sherry on page 135*).

The Vergine and Solera wines are not sweetened and can be very pleasant aperitifs. Most sweet Marsala is used in the kitchen.

SARDINIA

Sardinia makes a fair amount of wine, covering the whole gamut of styles. The wine that has had most success on the export markets is the dry white, DOCG Vermentino di Gallura. The best examples have a good blast of ripe peachy fruit and decent balancing acidity.

Fact Box

Age indications of Marsala

Fine: 1 year.
Superiore: 2 years.
Superiore Reserva: 4 years.
Vergine or Solera: 5 years.
Vergine Stravecchio or Reserva (and Solera Stravecchio or Reserva): 10 years.

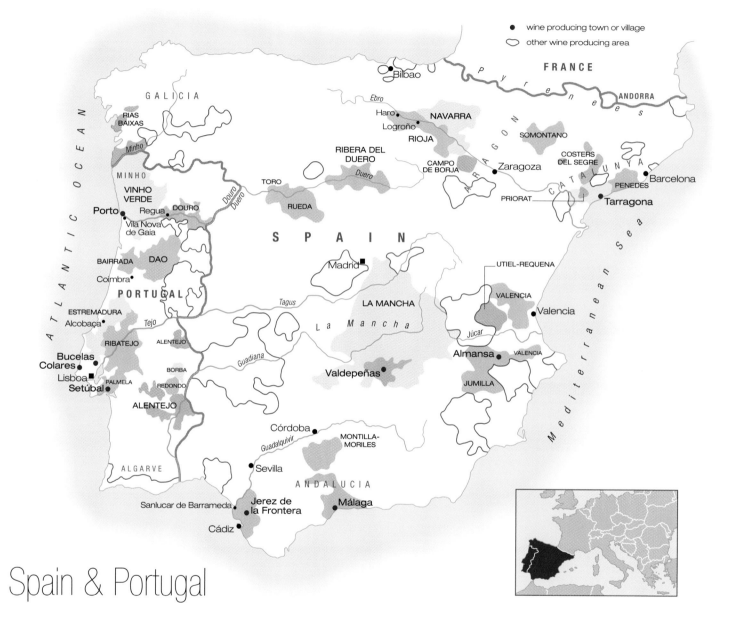

wine producing town or village

other wine producing area

FRANCE

ANDORRA

GALICIA

RIAS BAIXAS

Bilbao

Ebro

Haro

Logroño

NAVARRA

RIOJA

SOMONTANO

Zaragoza

COSTERS DEL SEGRE

CATALUNYA

Barcelona

PENEDES

Tarragona

PRIORAT

RIBERA DEL DUERO

Duero

TORO

RUEDA

Minho

MINHO

VINHO VERDE

Porto

Regua

DOURO

Vila Nova de Gaia

Douro

S P A I N

Madrid

UTIEL-REQUENA

VALENCIA

BAIRRADA

DAO

Coimbra

P O R T U G A L

Tagus

LA MANCHA

Valencia

Júcar

VALENCIA

ESTREMADURA

Alcobaça

Tejo

La   Mancha

ALENTEJO

Almansa

RIBATEJO

Bucelas

Colares

Lisboa

Setúbal

PALMELA

BORBA

REDONDO

Guadiana

Valdepeñas

JUMILLA

ALENTEJO

Córdoba

MONTILLA-MORILES

ALGARVE

Guadalquivir

Sevilla

A N D A L U C I A

Sanlucar de Barrameda

Jerez de la Frontera

Málaga

Cádiz

ATLANTIC OCEAN

Mediterranean Sea

Pyrenees

ARAGON

The world of wine

Spain & Portugal

In the past, Spanish light wine was often dismissed as the lowest of the low, as exemplified by 'Spanish Sauternes' and 'Spanish Chablis'. However, both standard and reputation have improved markedly in recent years. Portugal's light wine renaissance is also well under way, with some real gems for the assiduous drinker to track down.

SPAIN

Spain has the largest area of land under vine in the world. Yet in terms of volume of wine actually produced it comes only third after France and Italy. The reason for this anomaly is that average vineyard yields are very low in Spain. The arid climate in central Spain, combined with the ban on irrigation (this is relaxed under exceptional circumstances), naturally restricts the crop that each vine can produce.

Spanish wine law

The Spanish have a similar four-stage classification to that found elsewhere in the EU.

Vino de Mesa

This is Spain's basic table wine, equivalent to Vin de Table in France.

Vino de la Tierra / Vino Comarcal

These are upmarket Table Wines that indicate whereabouts in Spain they come from. They are roughly equivalent to the French Vin de Pays.

Denominación de Origen (DO)

DO is the lower level of quality wine in Spain. The parallel French designation is VDQS. However, given the importance of DO in Spain (there are over 50 such regions), Italy's DOC category is a more relevant comparison.

Denominación de Origen Calificada (DOCa)

This category is reserved for Spain's top wines. So far Rioja is the only wine accorded this status. Being the highest grade of Spanish wine it is equivalent to Appellation Contrôlée (or DOCG).

Maturation designations

As well as stating their quality status and origin, many Spanish wines will also indirectly indicate the length of time they were matured before release. There are four age designations (*see chart on page 128*). One slight quirk is that the DOCa rules for Rioja specify a minimum of one year in oak for a Crianza, rather than the national rule of just six months.

The wine regions of Spain

There are huge climatic variations across Spain. The region of Galicia in the north-west of the country faces the Atlantic Ocean and therefore has a mild, humid climate. By contrast, La Mancha, right in the centre of Spain, is dry and

From left to right: a Crianza, a Reserva and a Gran Reserva Rioja.

Age rules applied to red wines

Age designation	Vino Joven (or Sin Crianza)	Crianza	Reserva	Gran Reserva
Minimum maturation time in oak	Nil.	6 months.	1 year.	2 years.
Minimum total maturation time	Nil.	2 years.	3 years.	5 years.

The world of wine

experiences some drastic extremes of temperature. Altitude also has a big influence on the climate of many of Spain's vineyard areas.

DOCa RIOJA

For many people Rioja was, and still is, synonymous with good Spanish red wine. Rioja in the past was also a bargain relative to many of the Old World's other classic wines. However, the world has moved on, prices have gone up and there are now at least a dozen 'new' regions of Spain that are producing some very impressive wines. In some circles today Rioja is viewed as over-priced and passé.

The emergence of boutique wines

One relatively recent development has been the emergence of 'boutique' super-premium Riojas. Rather than large-scale blends, these 'new wave' Riojas are often the product of a single estate. With more extraction during and after the fermentation, followed by maturation in new French oak,

Best Buy

Rioja Gran Reserva, Paternina 1993

Mid-deep mahogany core. Mid brick rim. The bouquet is mellow and smooth, with savoury, peaty notes coming through. Figs and prunes. Also some creamy oak. Dry, low acidity, mid-alcohol. Mid-bodied. The tannins are very rounded. Soft and harmonious on the palate. Quite a long finish.

these wines are much more 'international' than Spanish. In some cases the quality is impressive, although having been made in a 'Bordeaux-esque' way they can be rather raw and tannic when released.

Grape varieties in Rioja

As well as the famous reds (Tintos), Rioja also makes some rosés (Rosados) and dry whites (Blancos). The rosés can be pleasant when young, although neighbouring Navarra is better known for this style. Most white Rioja is technically correct, but very bland. One or two people do still age their whites in oak, but most producers go for a cold fermentation and early bottling.

The key black grape grown in the region is Tempranillo. When young, Tempranillo wines can have an attractive broad aroma of dark berries. Oak melds in well with these nuances. Although not particularly tannic, the best Tempranillo wines can age gracefully both in wood and bottle. Other black grapes are traditionally used to make up the blend. The Garnacha (Grenache) provides a warm, immediate softness that is particularly important in the early drinking, inexpensive Riojas. Graciano and Mazuelo (Carignan) are the other two local grape varieties that can add a dash of complexity.

Viura, overwhelmingly neutral in quality, is the main white grape. A little bit of Malvasia is grown as well.

The Rioja region is divided up into three main districts: Rioja Alta, Rioja Alavesa and Rioja Baja. Alta and Alavesa have moderate climates and produce most of the premium Riojas. Baja is

The dramatic setting of the Priorat vineyards in Catalunya.

hotter and the location of most of the Garnacha vineyards. Haro and Logroño are the towns where many of the wineries (*bodegas*, literally 'warehouses' or 'cellars') are located.

DO NAVARRA

Lying just north-east of Rioja, this region was for a long time associated with the production of cheap, quaffing rosés. Garnacha was the key grape. The move over the last couple of decades has been more towards red wines. A lot of

Tempranillo has been planted, along with French varieties like Cabernet Sauvignon and Merlot. Chardonnay has also been planted to help perk up the Viura-based whites. Navarra is often compared favourably with Rioja for being more innovative and sensibly priced.

DO CAMPO DE BORJA

Campo de Borja makes some inexpensive, fruity, spicy red wines that are fantastic for everyday swigging. Garnacha is the main grape variety.

The world of wine

Vines in the Toro region of north-west Spain.

DO SOMONTANO

This is a much talked about region in Aragón, lying in between Zaragoza and the Pyrenees. It produces reds and dry whites from both native (Garnacha, Tempranillo and Macabeo) and imported (Cabernet Sauvignon, Merlot, Chardonnay and Gewürztraminer) grape varieties.

DO RIBERA DEL DUERO

This region, located due north of Madrid and straddling the River Duero, is making a number of massive red wines (which sell for massive prices). It is the home of Spain's most famous wine estate, Vega Sicilia. Recently, big money has gone into establishing boutique wineries aimed at producing world-class red wines. Cabernet

Sauvignon and Merlot have long been planted in the Ribera del Duero, along with the Tempranillo.

DO RUEDA

Although the Rueda region was originally known for its fortified wines, its reputation today is based on the production of light, crisp, dry white wines. The local white grape, Verdejo, is still used alongside the recently planted Sauvignon Blanc.

DO TORO

Toro is best known for its hearty red wines based on the ubiquitous Tempranillo.

DO RIAS BAIXAS

This area is located in the extreme north-western corner of Spain, in the region of Galicia. With its temperate, maritime climate it specialises in the production of zippy, fresh, tart dry white wines. In fact, Rías Baixas is probably the most fashionable area of Spain for white wine production. The huge popularity of these wines on the domestic market can make them expensive for what they are. The star grape variety is the Albariño.

DO PENEDES

Directly west of Barcelona, this vineyard region is home base for the Torres winery, which has probably done more since the Second World War to establish Spain's credentials as a producer of quality wine than any other Spanish organisation. Penedés makes reds, whites and rosés using some native varieties like Macabeo (the local name for the Viura) and Ull de Llebre (Tempranillo in disguise). The region also has large plantings of imported grape varieties such as Chardonnay and Cabernet Sauvignon (plus some more exotic things like Gewürztraminer and Pinot Noir). Altitude is a crucial factor in Penedés – vineyards near the Mediterranean have a much hotter climate than those planted inland at up to 800 m (2625 ft).

DO CAVA

The same region of Catalunya that produces the still DO Penedés wines also grows most of the grapes for Spain's sparkling wines. The DO Cava is strange in not being restricted just to Penedés, but covering other regions of Spain including Rioja and Navarra. Cava is made by the traditional method (*método tradicional*), as outlined on page 62. The local white grapes are Parrelada, Xarel.lo and Macabeo, with Chardonnay now used by some companies. Monastrell (Mourvèdre) and Garnacha are used in the production of the rosé Cavas. The minimum maturation time on the yeast specified by the DO is nine months.

DO COSTERS DEL SEGRE

Costers del Segre lies on the western edge of Catalunya, close to the border with Aragón. This remote and arid area has become known to the outside world through the quality of the wines produced at the Raimat estate. The futuristic winery at the estate produces reds (using Cabernet Sauvignon, Merlot and Tempranillo), dry whites and sparkling wines (both from Chardonnay).

DO TARRAGONA

DO Tarragona is a large region producing relatively simple reds, rosés and dry whites. As well as Tempranillo, Garnacha and Cariñena (Carignan) are important black grape varieties. The white grape line-up includes the usual Catalan suspects: Parrelada, Xarel.lo and Macabeo.

DO PRIORAT

'Thinking man's rocket fuel' perhaps sums up what Priorat is all about. If you like your red wines big and rich, Priorat is for you. This small region is located inland from Tarragona, with the best vineyards high up, 700 m (2297 ft), around the village of Gratallops. The climate is hot and dry; the soils are slate and schist; the principal grapes are Garnacha, Cariñena, Cabernet Sauvignon and Syrah. These vineyard factors, combined with investment in the winery and some talented winemaking, have turned Priorat into Spain's cult red wine area.

DO LA MANCHA

La Mancha is the vast plain directly south of Madrid. Along with its neighbouring areas like Valdepeñas, this region of Spain accounts for roughly half of the country's wine production. Whilst quality improvements have been made, DO La Mancha is still primarily a producer of cheap and cheerful wines. The region has an extreme continental climate, with summer temperatures above 40°C (104°F) and winter temperatures below -20°C (-4°F) not unknown. Rainfall is very light as well. In the past the region was best known for its dry whites made from the Airén grape. However, some decent reds are now being produced from the Tempranillo.

Best Buy

Rueda, Marqués de Riscal 2000

Very pale straw. Clean as a whistle. Crisp, fresh simple fruit. Lemon and peardrops. Almost sappy. Dry, mid-acidity, moderate alcohol. Light-bodied. Delicate fruit. Shortish finish.

DO VALDEPENAS

DO Valdepeñas is in effect an enclave in the southern extremities of La Mancha. Its spicy, juicy reds show just what can be achieved in central Spain in spite of the desperate climate. The black grape grown in the region is Cencibel (our old friend Tempranillo, yet again).

DO ALMANSA

If Valdepeñas is La Mancha's southern enclave, Almansa is its eastern. DO Almansa makes some lovely, smooth red wines. As well as Tempranillo, the blend used in a red Almansa may well include Monastrell and Garnacha Tintorera.

DO JUMILLA

DO Jumilla lies south-east of La Mancha, but still experiences quite an extreme, arid climate. The quality of the region's red wines has been improving for a number of years. Monastrell is the key grape in Jumilla.

DO UTIEL-REQUENA

DO Utiel-Requena produces simple reds and decent rosés from the local black grape, Bobal.

DO VALENCIA

Most of the wine selling as DO Valencia is pretty basic stuff. Red, white and rosé wines are produced. The principal local white grape is the Merseguera, with Monastrell important for the reds. Often, the region's most attractive wine is Moscatel de Valencia. This sweet fortified white wine has an attractive, perfumed and raisiny aroma.

DO MONTILLA-MORILES

DO Montilla-Moriles is located in Andalucía, just south of Córdoba. In Britain, Montilla is known as a wine made in the Sherry mould, but cheaper. This is because most of the Montilla shipped to the UK has not been fortified, so it pays less duty than Sherry. It is produced in the same styles as Sherry (*see page 134*), with flor and oxidation being used to develop the wines' characteristics in the same way that they are in Jerez. The solera system is also utilised for the maturation and blending. Instead of Palomino though, the key grape in Montilla-Moriles is Pedro Ximénez.

DO MALAGA

Our distant ancestors drank quite a lot of 'Mountain', as Málaga was called in the past. With the decline in interest in most fortified wines and the urbanisation of the region around Málaga, production of this once important wine has declined sharply. However, it remains one of the world's great fortified wines. Although lighter and drier versions exist, the finest Málagas are rich and lusciously sweet. The solera system is sometimes used for maturation. The grape varieties used are Pedro Ximénez and Moscatel.

SHERRY (DO JEREZ-XERES-SHERRY)

Sherry is Spain's finest and most distinctive wine. Former generations had a proper appreciation of its great qualities. Sadly nowadays, the image of Sherry has been allowed to slip badly. In export markets like the UK sales declined sharply at the end of the twentieth century. There has been talk

The extraordinary *albariza* soil of the Jerez region.

of a revival of interest at various stages, but getting a younger generation of wine drinkers to give Sherry a try is a struggle. I just hope that eventually consumers will realise that Sherry is the world's most undervalued and under-priced wine.

The Sherry region takes its name from the town of Jerez de la Frontera, which lies in between Sevilla and Cadiz. Many of the big Sherry companies are based in Jerez, and it is in the town's bodegas that most Sherries will mature. One special type of Sherry, Manzanilla, is matured in the coastal town of Sanlucar de Barrameda. The Sherry vineyards are located all around Jerez on gently undulating hills.

The climate in this part of Andalucía is very hot and dry. Rainfall occurs only during the winter months (October to March). For the whole growing season, through the searing heat of summer, the vines have to survive on whatever moisture they can find in the soil. The special type of soil that furnishes the moisture is the striking 'albariza'. Brilliant white in colour, with a very high lime content, the *albariza* absorbs the winter rain and takes on a paste-like consistency. In the spring the surface of the *albariza* bakes into a crust. The soil beneath stays moist and provides the vines with the water they need during the summer. There are some clay and sand soils but they are less good.

The world of wine

The main styles of Sherry

Fino
Pale coloured, with a pungent yeasty 'flor' aroma, a standard Fino will be dry and light-bodied on the palate. Fino Sherries should always be drunk chilled. Fino Sherry becomes stale quite quickly, so never have more than a bottle or two in the house. Once opened, the purists would say that a Fino needs to be drunk up within a couple of weeks.

Pale Cream
This is a Fino that has been sweetened up through the addition of concentrated must.

Manzanilla
The lightest and palest of all the Sherries, with even more flor bite than a Fino. Like a Fino, Manzanilla should be served chilled. Being dry and fresh, Manzanilla can be an excellent accompaniment to grilled fish.

Amontillado
An aged, dry Amontillado is one of the most complex of all the Sherries. The nose can have an almost overwhelming complexity and the length of flavour on the finish sometimes lasts for minutes.

Medium
A commercial Medium Sherry is a cheapish Amontillado that has been sweetened up.

Oloroso
Old, dry Oloroso is an awesomely mellow wine, with layers of fragrance and richness on the nose. Deep but dry on the palate, it is another style capable of great length on the finish.

Cream
Sweetening up an Oloroso gives a Cream Sherry. The best Cream Sherries will be sweetened with PX sweetening wine.

Palo Cortado
This rare, dry Sherry combines some of the finest traits of an Amontillado and an Oloroso. A good example is fantastically complex and harmonious.

Pedro Ximénez
A small amount of the PX sweetening wine is bottled and sold in its own right. Dark, raisiny and rich, death by osmotic shock awaits anyone who risks a second glass.

The production process
The main grape planted in the Sherry region is the Palomino. A little Pedro Ximénez (often referred to as 'PX') and Moscatel are grown, but these are used to make sweetening wines only.

The Palomino is picked by hand in September. The grapes are crushed and pressed, the juice fermented, and a normal, neutral dry white wine is produced. This wine has an alcohol content of around 12%ABV. Grape spirit (at around 54%ABV) is added to the base wine and its alcohol content is pushed up to 15.5%ABV. This gently fortified wine then goes into large oak barrels, or 'butts', with a capacity of 550 litres (145 US gallons) to start its maturation. One of Sherry's many quirks is that the butts are never filled to the top and they are never sealed with a bung either.

After a few months in the butts, the cellar master will take a sample of wine from each barrel and usually based on the aroma alone, will classify the wines as either Finos or Olorosos.

Fino and flor
The Finos are left at 15.5%ABV. These butts naturally become infected with a strain of yeast called 'flor'. These yeast form a layer across the surface of the wine, almost like a white scum. The yeast feed on the wine, altering its composition and giving the Fino its distinctive pungent aroma. What is more, the yeast form a barrier to the air, excluding oxygen and therefore preventing oxidation. As a result, the Finos retain their natural pale colour.

Most Finos are matured in Jerez and turn into 'regular' Fino Sherry. The Fino butts in Jerez grow flor for most of the year, but the yeast do die back a bit in the summer heat. If a Fino is matured in the milder, coastal environment of Sanlucar de Barrameda, the yeast can grow year round. The resulting super-light and ultra-pale Sherry is called Manzanilla.

If a butt of Fino is left for an extended period of time, eventually the flor will use up all the nutrients in the wine. As the flor yeast die they sink to the bottom of the butt, exposing the surface to the atmosphere. The wine will darken in colour and the nose takes on a more complex, nutty character. This aged Fino is known as Amontillado. This process can be accelerated for the cheaper Amontillados by prematurely killing the flor through the addition of grape spirit.

The butts originally classified as Olorosos have a little extra grape spirit added, pushing their alcohol content up to 17.5%ABV. Flor cannot cope with this alcoholic strength, so there is no protective yeast layer on the surface of an Oloroso. Hence the Olorosos undergo long-term oxidation, becoming dark in colour and rich in flavour. Occasionally a butt of Sherry is noticed that is lighter and more refined than a standard Oloroso. This rarity is called Palo Cortado.

The solera system

Having generated the 'working' styles of Sherry (Fino, Manzanilla, Amontillado, Oloroso and Palo Cortado), the next stage is to start to blend these individual butts of wine with other butts of the same style. This is achieved through the famous solera system. When confronted by a solera on a bodega visit all you tend to see is what looks like a wall of butts. Three or four layers of barrels are stacked on top of each other. All of these butts

are partially filled with Sherry that is slowly maturing. When they want to bottle some Sherry they take wine out of the butts that are sitting on the ground (no more than a third of the volume of each butt per year). The cellar team then clamber up to the butts that are at shoulder height and siphon wine from these barrels into the ground level butts, returning the latter to their original fill level. Having completed that exercise the cellar team then climb up to the third layer of butts and siphon wine from there to top up the barrels in the second row. This process goes on until the team reach the top of the solera, at which stage the young wines are fed in.

Each style of Sherry has its own soleras. In other words, a young Fino will be fed into a Fino solera, a young Oloroso into an Oloroso solera and so on. It is worth bearing in mind that some of these soleras have been in operation for many decades. What this means is that the wine coming off the bottom will be a blend of every year going back to the setting up of the solera.

Blending and bottling

Once a Sherry has been through the solera system it needs to be prepared for bottling. A big brand cannot be entirely sourced from one solera, so a final blend is put together from various soleras. After fining and filtration many Sherries are bottled dry. However, several styles of Sherry need to be sweetened up. The best sweetening wine is produced from the Pedro Ximénez grape variety. The PX grapes are picked as normal, but are then laid out in the sun on mats. They quickly raisin. These raisined grapes are pressed,

The world of wine

The hand harvesting of high trained vines in the Vinho Verde region.

releasing a heroically sweet juice. This is prevented from fermenting by the addition of grape spirit. The best PX sweetening wines are passed through the solera system just like a normal Sherry. The required amount of sweetening wine is then added to the final blend. The sweetness in cheaper, paler Sherries is achieved through the addition of concentrated must.

Egg white or bentonite fining, cold treatment (tartrate stabilisation) and filtration precede the bottling. Finally, grape spirit may be added to get the Sherry to its required bottling strength.

PORTUGAL

In terms of vineyard area and volume of wine produced, Portugal is obviously dwarfed by its neighbour on the Iberian Peninsula. However, it is by no means a small wine producer. Yet, with the exception of its fortified wines and a few warhorse brands, Portuguese wines are not that well known on the export markets.

In the past a lot of Portuguese red wine was made in a rather hard, earthy style, with marked underlying acidity and green tannins. The whites were often flat and verging on oxidised. Happily, things are now changing for the better.

Portuguese wine law

The Portuguese now have the standard EU four-category system for classifying their wines.

Vinho de Mesa

This is Portugal's basic Table Wine, equivalent to Vin de Table in France. The most famous Vinho de Mesa wines are the medium dry, slightly sparkling, rosés (Mateus and Lancers).

Vinho Regional

One step up from Vinho de Mesa is Vinho Regional, the Portuguese answer to Vin de Pays.

Indicação de Proveniência Regulamentada (IPR)

This is the lower level of quality wine in Portugal. It is comparable to France's VDQS.

Denominação de Origem Controlada (DOC)

DOC (not to be confused with the Italian category) is Portugal's top-quality designation.

Garrafeira

Like in Spain, there is a tradition in Portugal of maturing wines (particularly reds) for an extended period in wood and bottle before release. A red

'Garrafeira', as well as having to have an alcohol content at least half a percent above the legal minimum, must be matured in wood for at least two years and in bottle for at least one year.

The wine regions of Portugal

For a relatively small country, Portugal has marked variations of climate from north to south and west to east. The Algarve and Alentejo in the south have an almost Mediterranean climate. By contrast, the Minho region in the north-west (home to Vinho Verde), is cooler, wetter and distinctly Atlantic in its climate. Venture inland from there, up the Douro Valley for 100 km (63 miles) and the extreme dry, continental climate experienced by central Spain takes over.

Another huge source of diversity in Portugal is its incredible patrimony of native grape varieties. Only in relatively recent years have the Portuguese growers and research institutes started to get to grips with the characteristics of some of the best of these varieties. If the world does get sick of Cabernet Sauvignon and Merlot, then Portugal is well placed to supply wines made from high quality esoteric grape varieties (either as varietals or blends). However, in the short term, there is the challenge of selling wines made from unfamiliar varieties. 'Darling, do try this Trincadeira Preta. I like it even more than the Castelão Françês' is hardly a commonplace dinner party line.

DOC VINHO VERDE

In the past, Vinho Verde was most people's introduction to Portuguese white wine. Dry or medium dry, with lightish alcohol and high acidity, many of these standard Vinhos Verdes also have a slight *pétillance*. The vineyards in the extreme north of Portugal, up by the Spanish border close to the River Minho, produce the best examples of Vinho Verde. The main grape up there is the Alvarinho. A significant amount of red Vinho Verde is produced for the home market.

DOC DOURO

The Douro Valley is of course best known for the production of Port (*see page 138*). However, there has been a growing interest in the making of premium red wines. The best examples have plenty of deep plummy fruit, overlaid with new oak.

DOC DAO

Dão remains Portugal's most famous red wine region. Whilst many of the wines are still rather tough and leathery, there are some quintas (wine estates) making cleaner, fruit-driven wines. The region lies some distance inland, with vineyards planted as high as 500 m (1640 ft). The soils are granitic. The black grape line-up includes Touriga Nacional, Alfrocheiro Preto, Jaen, Tinta Roriz (Tempranillo) and Tinta Cão. Some dry white Dão is now made from the Encruzado grape variety.

DOC BAIRRADA

With Bairrada you can experience the extremes of wine quality. There is still a lot of thin, hard, mediocre wine produced in Bairrada. By contrast, in the shape of Luis Pato, the region is home to one of Portugal's star winemakers. The Bairrada vineyards lie in between Dão and the sea, just north of the university town of Coimbra. The key to

The world of wine

Best Buy

Dão, Terras Altas, J. M. Fonseca 1997

Mid-deep garnet core. Mid-brick rim. Touches of complexity on the nose. Earthy, leathery and vegetal. Dried fruits. Dry, mid-low acidity, moderate alcohol. Mid-full bodied. Chewy and savoury on the mid-palate. Some fleshy tannins. Mid-length. Drinking well now and will keep for a couple of years.

Bairrada is the Baga grape variety. It is a cussed character, prone to over-cropping, uneven ripening and tart acidity. However, with fanatical care in the vineyard and cellar, it can produce deeply concentrated wines capable of long maturation.

ESTREMADURA

This coastal region runs north from Lisboa to Alcobaça. It is Portugal's largest wine producing area. Much of the wine is simple and unsophisticated. However, there are some wineries making approachable, modern-style wines at reasonable prices. DOC Bucelas is a small, dry white wine producing district just outside Lisboa. DOC Colares is also close to the capital and is famous for its austere red wines produced from ungrafted vines.

DOC RIBATEJO

Like its neighbour Estremadura, Ribatejo is traditionally a producer of simple wines. A lot of the bulk wine vineyards have been grubbed up since the 1980s. The remaining growers and wineries are increasingly aiming for better quality.

DOC SETUBAL

Moscatel de Setúbal is Portugal's great unsung vinous treasure. Trendy mock New World wines may be all the rage, but Setúbal is a timeless classic. It is a fortified Muscat wine produced just south of Lisboa. The young versions are soft and grapey, with hints of dried apple and orange peel on the nose. With age the wines develop an awesome richness and complexity, the bouquet exhibiting toffee, chocolate and raisin nuances. The light wine DOC Palmela covers much the same ground as Setúbal. Some honest, supple reds are made from the Castelão Francês.

DOC ALENTEJO

The vast, baked rolling landscape of Alentejo has a different feel from the countryside in north and central Portugal. Until recently the region was viewed as capable of producing only humble wines. Big investment though, over the last 20 years, has turned Alentejo into Portugal's trendiest wine region. Cabernet Sauvignon and Syrah join local black grapes Tinta Roriz (sometimes called Aragonês), Trincadeira Preta and Castelão Francês. Native white grapes include Antão Vaz, Arinto and Roupeiro. The region is sub-divided into smaller DOCs including Borba and Redondo.

PORT

Portugal's light wines may have had their ups and downs, but in Port the country has one of the world's great wines. The Port industry is centred around the River Douro in northern Portugal. The DOC Porto (Port is the anglicism) vineyards are nowhere near the city of Porto. They start 80 km (50 miles) inland from Porto near the town of Regua and run upstream to the Spanish border. The rugged mountainous country between the vineyards of the 'Upper Douro' and the coast cuts out much of the maritime influence. Hence the Upper Douro has an extreme climate, with cool winters and hot summers. Rainfall is relatively light.

Slopes and grapes

The vineyards of the Upper Douro are some of the most stunningly beautiful in the world. The River

Douro has cut a deep gorge through the hard schistous rocks of the region. This has forced generations of workers to build dramatic terraces on the steep slopes.

The wine producing farms of the Upper Douro are known as 'quintas' (as they are throughout Portugal). Most of the large Port shipping firms own one or more quintas. However, the shippers are dependent on smaller growers for a significant proportion of their grape requirement.

Like most of Portugal's other wine regions, the Upper Douro is blessed (or cursed?) with a bewildering number of grape varieties. Most of them are black; the principal examples are Tinta Barroca, Touriga Francesa, Tinta Amarela, Tinta Roriz, Touriga Nacional and Tinta Cão.

The production process

The grapes are picked by hand in September or October. They are transported to the wineries at the quintas. The grapes are crushed (a significant proportion of the top-quality grapes is still trodden in stone troughs called 'lagares') and a normal red wine fermentation starts.

Port production starts to deviate from normal red winemaking half-way through the fermentation. After between two and four days, roughly half the sugar will have been converted into alcohol (the fermenting wine will be around 6%ABV). At this moment the vat or lagar is drained. As the wine drains out it is mixed with grape spirit (water white neutral brandy) that is 77%ABV (capable of raising the dead). If the proportions are roughly four parts fermenting wine to one part spirit the mixture should come out at about 20%ABV. The

yeast die at this concentration of alcohol so the fermentation is arrested, leaving a sweet red wine. The raw young Port is then transferred to vats or barrels to start its maturation.

Pipes and lodges

The traditional barrels for maturing Port are called 'pipes' and have a capacity of around 550 litres (145 US gallons). In the past all the pipes of Port bound for the export market were moved out of the Upper Douro and taken down river to the town

Quinta do Noval, one of the leading estates in the Upper Douro region.

The world of wine

Fact Box

Port styles
Vintage.
Single Quinta Vintage.
LBV.
Colheita.
Tawny.
10 Year Old Tawny.
20 Year Old Tawny.
30 Year Old Tawny.
40+ Year Old Tawny.
Ruby.
Vintage Character Ruby.
Crusted Port.
White Port.

Port styles. From left to right:
Vintage, Single Quinta Vintage,
LBV, Indicated Age Tawny,
Standard Ruby and
Standard Tawny.

of Vila Nova de Gaia to complete their maturation. The warehouses, which are crammed together overlooking the river, are known as 'lodges'.

The evolution of Port styles

During its maturation in wood Port behaves like any other red wine. If it spends a short time in pipe the wine will retain its vibrant colour and dark fruit aromas. This is the origin of the Ruby family of Ports. By contrast, with extended wood maturation the colour will fade to an orangey-brown and the bouquet will develop mellow, woody, raisiny notes. This gives rise to Tawny Ports.

The evolution of the wines in wood, and the quality of the grapes to start with, are the origins of the main categories of Port.

Vintage Port

This is a wine of one year, e.g. Warre 1977. Vintage Ports are traditionally made only in really exceptional years, perhaps three times a decade. The decision whether to make a Vintage Port lies with each Port producer (subject to approval by the Instituto do Vinho do Porto – IVP). It is usually made in only small quantities, and is often a blend of the finest pipes from several properties.

The wine destined to be a Vintage Port is matured for two to three years in wood (barely longer than a normal red wine). It is then bottled without fining and filtration. This Vintage Port then needs to be laid down for 20 years. During this extended maturation the wine will smooth out and throw a heavy sediment ('crust') – hence the need to decant a Vintage Port. Although 20 years is the time required by a Vintage Port to reach its prime, once there it can stay in fine form for another 20 years or more in some cases.

Single Quinta Vintage Port

There are always some harvests when the quality of the wines is good, but not quite good enough to make a 'full' Vintage Port, e.g. 1986. What many Port Houses do nowadays is to bottle a little Vintage Port from that year, but just using wines

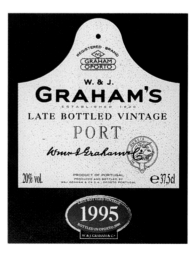

from one of their top Quintas. So instead of the wine appearing as 'Dow 1985', what you will come across is 'Dow, Quinta do Bomfim 1986'. These wines are popular with the Port cognoscenti for two important reasons. Firstly, they generally mature in bottle more quickly than a full Vintage Port and therefore do not need to be laid down for so long. Secondly, they are usually half the price of a full Vintage Port.

Late Bottled Vintage Port (LBV)

Like a Vintage Port, an LBV is a wine of one year, e.g. Taylor's Late Bottled Vintage 1995. However, unlike Vintage Ports, LBVs are made in most years and in large volumes. LBVs are matured in wood for twice as long (four to six years) as Vintage Ports. Most LBVs are fined and filtered before bottling. This treatment, along with the longer maturation in wood, means that LBVs do not throw a sediment. What is more, they are ready to drink when shipped and require no further bottle maturation. A few Port Houses do make 'traditional-style' LBV, which has not been fined and may throw a sediment.

Colheita (Date of Harvest) Port

Again this is a wine of one year, but instead of being bottled after a relatively short time in wood, it is matured in pipe for at least eight years. The Colheita develops into a complex, mellow, tawny wine. Any sediment will fall out during the period in wood. Hence upon bottling the wines are ready to drink and do not need decanting.

Indicated Age Tawny Port

Rather than being the product of one year, these Ports are a combination of wines from several years. All will have received extended maturation in wood before blending and bottling. Like the Colheita, any potential crust-forming material will have settled out during the years in pipe. Again like a Colheita, these harmonious and rounded Ports are ready to drink when shipped. The Indicated Age Tawnies come in four age levels:

Fact Box

The main years for Vintage Port since the Second World War

1945, 1947, 1948, 1950, 1955, 1960, 1963, 1966, 1970, 1975, 1977, 1980, 1983, 1985, 1991, 1994, 1997.

Although at the time of writing nobody will say anything officially, the 2000 harvest in the Upper Douro, though small, was of exceptional quality.

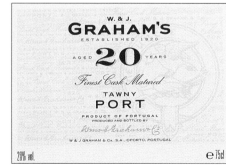

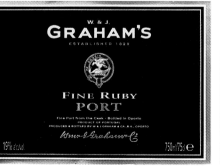

The rugged and remote
Upper Douro Valley.

10 Year Old, 20 Year Old, 30 Year Old and 40+ Year Old, representing the approximate age of the blend. Indicated Age Tawnies remain good value for money, particularly for drinkers who find the Vintage and LBV styles a bit raw and fiery.

White Port

White Port is generally pretty simple stuff. It is made in the same sort of way as red Port, but using some of the Upper Douro's white grape varieties. White Port will normally receive a short period in wood, perhaps two to three years, before blending and bottling. Some white Ports are fully sweet, whilst others are made in a drier style. White Port should be drunk chilled as an apéritif.

Ruby Port

A standard Ruby will be blended on a large scale from young red Ports. It will probably mature only for about three years before fining, filtration and bottling. A normal Ruby can be a bit coarse and jammy.

Many Port Houses now also make an 'up-market' Ruby. This will be a superior blend to that used for the standard Ruby, and will spend slightly longer in wood (around four or five years). The most famous of these is Cockburn's Special Reserve. Rather confusingly, these glorified Rubies are often labelled as 'Vintage Character'.

If an upmarket Ruby is bottled without fining and filtration it will throw a sediment in the same sort of way as a Vintage Port. This style is referred to as 'Crusted Port'.

Tawny Port

Standard Tawny Ports are normally fairly basic wines. Rather than having picked up their character from maturation in wood, many commercial Tawnies are just blends of red and white Ports.

MADEIRA

The beautiful island of Madeira is located in the Atlantic Ocean. It lies 1100 km (688 miles) south-west of Lisboa. Politically it is part of Portugal. The capital of the island is the large town of Funchal.

Being so far south (32° North) and surrounded by the ocean gives Madeira a gentle, sub-tropical climate. The mountains career up to nearly 1900 m (6234 ft). Most of the vineyards are on dramatic terraced sites on the south side of the island.

The production process

Madeira starts out as pretty ordinary white wine. Most will be fermented to dryness and then fortified with grape spirit (96%) bought in from Europe. Some of the sweeter versions will have the spirit added during the fermentation, rather like Port.

It is what happens next that gives Madeira its unique character. The young wines undergo a period of heating called 'estufagem'. The cheaper Madeiras are placed in vats, which are then heated to around 45°C (113°F) and the wine is held at that temperature for three months. This cooking process has a drastic effect on the wine, darkening its colour, giving the aroma a caramelised, raisiny character and lowering the wine's acidity. Rather than *estufagem* in vat, the finer Madeiras are winched up to the loft of the lodge and left to mature under the roof. This cooking is more gentle and may go on for several years (it is known as 'canteiro').

After *estufagem* the wines then mature in wood for anywhere between three and 70 years or more. This extended oxidative maturation, on top of the *estufagem*, makes Madeira almost indestructible. Bottles of Madeira from the nineteenth century are still drinking well today. What is more, Madeira will stay fresh in the bottle or decanter for months after opening.

Grapes and grades

The most important grape for Madeira production is the Tinta Negra Mole. This variety is used to make the standard three-year-old blends. These wines are often sweetened with rectified concentrated must (*see page 61*) and coloured with caramel. Much of this basic, cheap Madeira is used in cooking.

The finer Madeiras are made from the following varieties (which tend to equate to the indicated styles):

Sercial – dry.
Verdelho – medium dry.
Bual – medium sweet.
Malmsey – very sweet.

These top Madeiras may come in the form of Reserve (5 years old), Special Reserve (10 years old), Extra Reserve (15 years old) and Solera (*see page 135*) blends. The latter show the year the solera was started, e.g. Leacock's Sercial Solera 1860. The most extraordinary of the Madeiras are the vintage wines. These Madeiras have to mature in wood for at least 20 years before bottling, although many are kept for much longer. Cossart Gordon's Bual 1908 was bottled in 1985 after 77 years in oak. The concentration and complexity of such wines is awesome.

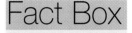

Fact Box

Top grades of Madeira

Reserve (5 years old),
Special Reserve (10 years old),
Extra Reserve (15 years old),
Solera (date Solera was started),
Vintage (date of vintage),

The world of wine

Above: Autumn at Denbies in Surrey, the largest vineyard in England. What would that Keats fellow have made of it? Far right: Steeply terraced vineyards overlooking Lake Geneva.

ENGLAND AND WALES

A word of explanation is needed to distinguish between English Wine and British Wine. English Wine is made from grapes that are grown in England. It is the product of fresh grapes and therefore complies with the EU definition of wine (*see page 32*). British Wine is made from imported grape juice concentrate (it is sometimes referred to as 'made wine'). Being made from a concentrate it falls outside the EU definition of wine. For this reason British Wine is governed by UK law. British Wine is produced in fortified and light wine styles. Also part of the British Wine family are Tonic Wine (where vitamins, herb extracts etc. have been added to a base wine) and Ginger Wine (fermented from raisins and stem ginger).

Vines have been spasmodically cultivated in what is now England since Roman times. However, today's commercial vineyards and wineries have been set up since the Second World War. Not surprisingly, most of these are located in the southern half of England. In particular, counties like Kent, Sussex, Surrey and Hampshire have quite a large number of vineyards. There are a handful of vineyards in Wales, hence the existence of Welsh Wine. The organisation representing the growers is the United Kingdom Vineyards Association (UKVA).

Cool climate dictates

The fundamental problem about wine production in England is the climate. Apart from the Lizard Peninsula in Cornwall, the whole of the English mainland lies beyond 50°N. The Gulf Stream does moderate the climate, but getting healthy, ripe grapes is always going to be a challenge. This means that even when the wines are successful they can never be particularly cheap.

The cool climate dictates that most English wine will be white, with high acidity and moderate alcohol. Chaptalisation is used to get the alcohol up to a decent level, and *süssreserve* is added to give sweetness. A few red and rosé wines are

made, but it is not easy to get black grapes ripe in English conditions. Some of the most interesting work is being done on sparkling wine production. With its cool climate and chalky soils, south-east England may have potential as a producer of traditional method sparkling wine.

Many of the early ripening German crosses have been planted in England, e.g. Müller-Thurgau, Reichensteiner, Ortega and Bacchus. The hybrid vine Seyval Blanc is also fairly widely planted. Chardonnay and Pinot Noir are grown as well, particularly for sparkling wine production.

Originally all the wine produced in England and Wales was classified just as Table Wine. There is now a Quality Wine scheme in place, based around a blind tasting appraisal.

LUXEMBOURG

Luxembourg is a small wine producer. Most of the wine produced there is drunk in the Grand Duchy itself, so very little is seen on the export market. With its cool climate and proximity to the Mosel Valley, it is no surprise that white wine dominates the production. The grape varieties planted include Müller-Thurgau (Rivaner) and Elbling.

SWITZERLAND

Switzerland makes attractive white and light-bodied red wines. Production is not large and the standard of living is very high making prices high, hence the limited exports. The French-speaking cantons (such as Vaud and Valais) account for most of the production. Chasselas (known as Fendant) is the most important white grape. Pinot Noir and Gamay are the key black varieties.

The world of wine

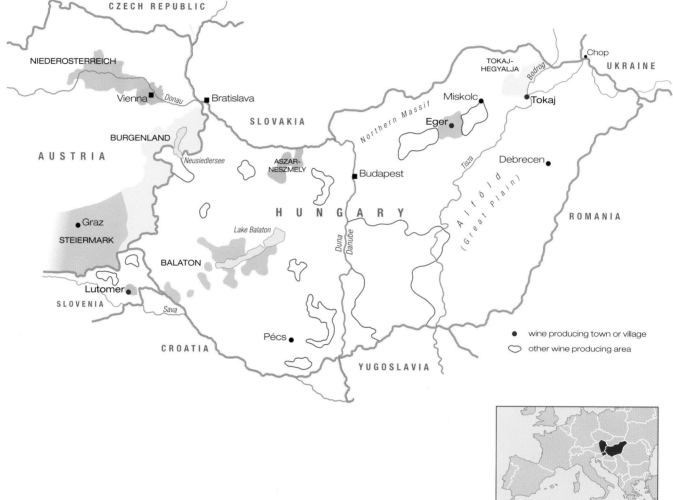

Central Europe

The wine producing countries of Central Europe have all had their challenges over the last 20 years: Austria the stigma of the 'anti-freeze' scandal, Hungary the huge structural changes that accompanied the end of Communism, Slovenia and the former Yugoslavia the horrors of civil war.

AUSTRIA

The Austrian wine industry has had to re-invent itself over the last 15 years. In 1985 diethylene glycol was discovered in several Austrian wines. The press turned this into the 'anti-freeze' scare, even though diethylene glycol is not anti-freeze and the quantities being added were so small that nobody suffered any ill effects. In fact, it was being used to make the wines seem richer and sweeter, so that they could be sold for a higher price. The wine law and its enforcement were subsequently tightened up and bit by bit the better wines are getting the sort of international recognition they deserve.

Like Germany, Austria is primarily a white wine producing country. However, Austria lies further south and further east than Germany. This gives Austria summers that are warmer and drier. Hence an average Austrian wine will tend to be higher in alcohol, lower in acidity and have slightly more body than its German cousin.

Grapes and styles

The most widely planted white grape in Austria is the Grüner Veltliner. This normally produces a fresh and spicy dry white wine. Müller-Thurgau and Welschriesling are grown and usually make fairly simple wines (although the latter does produce some interesting sweet wines). There are some very good wines made from Riesling and Gewürztraminer. Other local white grapes include: Bouvier, Neuburger, Rotgipfler and Spätrot.

Probably the most interesting of the local black grapes is the St. Laurent. It may be related to Pinot Noir and it is certainly capable of producing

wines with an attractive, soft fruitiness. Other black varieties grown in Austria include Blauer Portugieser, Blaufränkisch and Zweigelt.

The village of Lagenlois in Niederösterreich, Austria's largest vineyard region.

Austrian wine law

The Austrian wine law is very similar to that used in Germany (*see page 113*). The ripeness of the grapes at harvest time (determined by their sugar content) decides the quality level of the wine. Most of the categories are the same as in Germany. However, the Austrians have squeezed in a couple of extra Prädikatswein categories. 'Ausbruch' is a Noble Rot wine, with a qualifying sweetness level lying in between Beerenauslese and Trockenbeerenauslese. 'Strohwein' is a sweet white wine made from grapes that have been dried indoors (rather like the Vin de Paille made in the Jura region of France). Strohwein has to have the same minimum sugar content as Beerenauslese and Eiswein.

The wine regions of Austria

Most of the vineyards in Austria are located in the east of the country. The largest vineyard region is called Niederösterreich (Lower Austria). A lot of the Grüner Veltliner grows there, as does the best of the Austrian Riesling. There are vineyards in the suburbs of Vienna that produce a youthful quaffing wine called 'Heurige'. Right on the border with Hungary is the Burgenland region. The vineyards around a shallow lake called the Neusiedlersee are very prone to Noble Rot, hence the fame of Burgenland for its sweet white wines. Steiermark (Styria) is in the south of Austria on the border with Slovenia. The main grape variety grown there is the Welschriesling.

HUNGARY

Given that Hungary was the most economically liberal of the Eastern Bloc countries, its wine industry has been able to adapt well to the end of Communism. It has built a very successful export market for its inexpensive varietal wines. What is more, it has already gone a long way to re-establishing the reputation of Tokay as one of the world's great sweet white wines.

Hungary has a classic central European climate, with cold winters and hot, dry summers. The grape varieties are a mixture of the familiar and the truly bizarre: Chardonnay, Ezerjó, Furmint, Gewürztraminer, Hárslevelü, Irsai Olivér, Olasz

Rizling (Laski Rizling) and Muscat are the white varieties, with black varieties represented by Cabernet Sauvignon, Kadarka, Kékfrankos (Blaufränkisch) and Merlot.

The wine regions in the western half of Hungary (such as Balaton and Ászár-Neszmély) have been responsible for producing many of the 'new wave' varietal wines. A number of these have been made under the watchful eyes of 'flying winemakers' (*see page 169*). The Great Plain of south-eastern Hungary produces a lot of very basic wine that is not seen much on the export market. The Northern Massif is where Hungary's two most famous wines come from. 'Bulls Blood' (or 'Egri Bikaver') is a hairy, fullish-bodied red wine from the city of Eger. The main grape varieties used are the Kadarka and Kékfrankos.

Tokaji

Also in the Northern Massif is Eastern Europe's finest wine region, Tokaj-Hegyalja. Tokaji is often anglicised to Tokay. It is a white wine based on the Furmint, Hárslevelü and Muscat grape varieties. The simplest versions of Tokaji are dry white wines made from grapes picked at normal ripeness. These will sell under their varietal names, e.g. Tokaji Furmint.

Tokaji Szamorodni

Things start to get interesting when *Botrytis cinerea* appears on the scene. The autumn mists from the River Bodrog, combined with the sheltered position of the vineyards, often trigger Noble Rot. If there is a limited amount of Noble Rot, whole bunches of grapes will be picked. When these are pressed the juice will vary in sweetness depending on just how much Noble Rot there was. This 'as it comes' style is called Tokaji Szamarodni, and can be dry or sweet (*száraz*= dry, *édes* = sweet). During its maturation in wood the dry version of Szamarodni sometimes develops a layer of yeast on its surface, rather like the flor in Jerez.

Tokaji Aszú

With rampant Noble Rot the pickers will isolate the individual Noble Rot berries to make Tokaji Aszú. The Noble Rot berries are mashed up to make a sweet paste. The paste is then mixed with a small amount of normal dry white wine. The more paste that is added to the wine, the sweeter the Tokaji Aszú will be. The paste used to be added from hods called 'puttonyos', and the sweetness of Tokaji Aszú is still indicated by its *puttonyos* number. Four levels with increasing sugar levels are allowed: 3, 4, 5 and 6 *puttonyos*. Once the paste and wine have been allowed to macerate, the mixture of paste and wine is pressed. The resulting sweet white wine is then matured for at least three years in barrel.

Tokaji Eszencia

A tiny amount of mega-sweet syrup is produced from the oozings of the Noble Rot berries before they are mashed up. This liquid takes years to ferment, and may still be only 3%ABV when bottled or blended with other Tokaji wines. It is called Tokaji Eszencia and must mature in barrel for at least five years. Through long maturation in wood, many of the old Tokays have an oxidative nose. Like all of the world's great Noble Rot wines, a fine Tokaji Aszú or Eszencia can age gracefully in the bottle for decades.

CZECH REPUBLIC AND SLOVAKIA

Both the Czech Republic and Slovakia make small amounts of wine, mainly white. The grape varieties include Pinot Blanc and Müller-Thurgau.

The village of Tokaj, which gives its name to Hungary's great sweet white wine.

SLOVENIA AND THE FORMER YUGOSLAVIA

Within the former Yugoslavia, Slovenia was the republic that sold the most wine in markets like the UK. The town of Lutomer in particular is famous for growing the Laski Rizling grape. This variety produces a simple medium-dry white wine. The Laski Rizling is totally different from the Riesling that grows in Germany and Alsace. Laski Rizling crops up elsewhere in Eastern Europe, and is known as Olasz Rizling in Hungary and Welschriesling in Austria. The conflict in the region has obviously reduced exports to a trickle.

The world of wine

South-eastern Europe

Bulgaria has had a lot of success as a producer of inexpensive varietal wines, with Romania following in its footsteps. Greece produces everything from Retsina to fascinating estate wines. Cyprus now makes some reasonable light wines. Elsewhere around the Mediterranean fortunes are mixed, with wine production in North Africa in decline.

Bulgarian wine regions

- Northern Region
- Southern Region
- Eastern Region
- South-western Region
- Sub-Balkan Region

● wine producing town or village

◯ other wine producing area

MOLDOVA, UKRAINE, RUSSIA AND GEORGIA

The former Soviet Union, of which these republics were part, was a large wine producer (perhaps fourth or fifth largest in the world in the 1980s). The quality of most of the wines was wretched, not least because the wine industry was a long way down the list of investment priorities. With the disintegration of the Soviet Union, the successor republics are grappling with the challenge of turning their wine industries into viable enterprises. However, political and economic instability is limiting desperately needed external investment.

Most of the vineyards are planted near the Black Sea, so they enjoy quite a favourable climate. As well as local grapes like Rkatsiteli and Saperavi, there are plantings of more familiar varieties like Aligoté and Cabernet Sauvignon.

ROMANIA

Romania has the largest area of land under vine in Eastern Europe (excluding the former Soviet Union). Much of the wine is of simple quality and most of it is drunk locally. The quality potential is very good, but like many parts of the Balkans investment has been lacking in the past.

Romania has produced some decent, inexpensive Pinot Noirs, despite the notorious difficulty of growing this variety. Other black varieties grown include Cabernet Sauvignon and the local grape, Feteasca Neagra. Chardonnay and Pinot Gris feature amongst the white varieties, along with native grapes like Feteasca Alba, Grasa and Tamiioasa Romaneasca. Important wine regions in Romania are: Cotnari, Dealul Mare, Murfatlar and Tirnave.

The statue at the entrance of a Bulgarian winery. (I don't think Bacchus would have found her much fun.)

BULGARIA

It is probably fair to say that many drinkers in the UK were introduced to red wine, and Cabernet Sauvignon in particular, through drinking Bulgarian wine. Twenty years ago, honest, soft, quaffing Bulgarian Cabernet Sauvignon was just about the most affordable decent red wine available. The

The Dealul Mare region of Romania. Although there are some token vines in the foreground, I chose this photograph because I love Orthodox churches.

invested in the hardware of modern winemaking: stainless steel vats, refrigeration equipment, filters etc. Given the low production costs, it was these moves in the 1960s and 1970s that laid the foundation for Bulgaria's export successes.

The post-Communist era

Even before the official end of Communist rule, difficulties started to arise for the Bulgarian wine industry. Demand from the Soviet Union plummeted during the Gorbachev years. Many vineyards were uprooted. With the slow and painful adaptation of the Bulgarian economy to the free market, big challenges have confronted the wine producers. The availability of grapes tumbled at one stage as vineyards were abandoned or poorly tended. There have inevitably been a number of bankruptcies. Hopefully though, once this period of transition is over, there is no reason why Bulgaria should not emerge as a thoroughly modern, commercial wine producer.

As well as Chardonnay, other 'Western' white grapes planted in Bulgaria include Sauvignon Blanc, Gewürztraminer and Riesling. Local grapes include Dimiat and Misket. Rkatsiteli is also grown. There is some Pinot Noir, along with Cabernet Sauvignon and Merlot. Gamza, Mavrud and Melnik are three important local black varieties.

The wine regions of Bulgaria
Northern Region

This is the largest wine producing region in Bulgaria. It is famous for its Cabernet Sauvignon. Gamza is grown here as well. The climate is generally warm, with some moderation provided

punters in Britain were not slow to lock on to the good value for money such wines represented. Sales grew strongly in the 1980s. Although more recently Bulgaria has struggled to maintain its market share, it remains a major source of inexpensive, uncomplicated glugging wines.

During the Communist period the Bulgarian wine industry was organised to allow for the mass production of wine. Huge vineyards were planted with widely spaced rows and high trained vines, to allow for the passage of tractors and to make manual vineyard tasks easier. Many shrewd decisions were taken. Large tracts of classic grape varieties, like Chardonnay, Merlot and Cabernet Sauvignon, were planted. Serious money was

by the River Danube on the border with Romania. Important areas within the Northern Region include Suhindol, Svischtov and Russe.

Southern Region

The Southern Region is marginally warmer than the Northern Region. Merlot features strongly here, along with the Cabernet Sauvignon and Mavrud varieties. Sakar, Haskovo, Stambolovo, Oriachovitza and Assenovgrad are all areas in the Southern Region.

Eastern Region

The Eastern Region benefits from the cooling effect of the Black Sea. This is Bulgaria's premier white wine area and has significant plantings of Chardonnay. Areas within the Eastern Region include Schumen, Khan Krum and Novi Pazar.

South-western Region

This is famous for the robust red wine from Melnik (the name of the town and the grape used).

Sub-Balkan Region

This region produces simple wines from the Misket grape. Sliven is the most famous area.

Bulgarian wine law

The wine authorities in Bulgaria have developed a legal framework that has parallels with the categories encountered in the EU:

Country Wine

This is the Bulgarian answer to French Vin de Pays.

Declared Geographical Origin (DGO)

This is roughly equivalent to VDQS.

Controliran

This is the highest grade of wine in Bulgaria and therefore comparable with Appellation Contrôlée.

Reserve and Special Reserve

Like the similar designations in Italy and Spain, Reserve and Special Reserve wines have received extended maturation in wood.

GREECE

As in many aspects of Western Civilisation, the Ancient Greeks played a pivotal role in spreading the cultivation of the vine around the Mediterranean. As well as making wine, the Greeks wrote about wine and used it in their religious rituals. The Ancient Greeks even had their own god of wine, Dionysus (also known as Bacchus). Even in the modern degraded secular world our subconscious awareness that wine is more than fermented grapes owes a lot to the Ancient Greeks.

Greece enjoys a warm Mediterranean climate. However, there are some important variations. For instance, it is 750 km (469 miles) from Macedonia to Crete, the former having a climate influenced by the Balkan landmass, the latter being surrounded by the sea and only 300 km (188 miles) from Libya. Greece is very mountainous, so altitude can also have a significant effect on climate.

Although there have been plantings of fashionable 'international' grape varieties like Chardonnay and Cabernet Sauvignon, most vines grown in Greece are of local origin. The key white grapes include Assyrtiko, Rhoditis, Muscat and Savatiano. Some of the main black grapes are Agiorgitiko, Limnio, Mandelaria and Xynomavro.

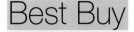

Best Buy

Bulgarian Cabernet Sauvignon, Domaine Boyar 1999

Mid-ruby core. Mid-ruby pink rim. Open textured and approachable, with simple dark fruit aromas. Dry, lowish acidity, mid-alcohol. Mid-bodied. Just a touch of stalky tannin. Uncomplicated, loose-knit fruit. Fairly short finish.

153

South-eastern Europe

The island of Samos is renowned for its Muscat wines.

resin to the fermenting white wine. In fact, the Ancients would have been very much at home with Retsina as they flavoured their wines with pitch, honey and herbs as well as resin. Modern Retsina has its own legal designation, Traditional Appellation (TA). Attica is the most famous region of Greece for Retsina production.

Even if one ignores Retsina, most of the wine made in Greece 20 years ago was poor. Since then there has been a change for the better. The large wine companies have drastically improved their winemaking and a number of boutique wineries have emerged making small amounts of impressive, concentrated wine. With its fascinating array of little-known local grapes, the premium end of the Greek wine industry is well placed to carve out a niche on the export market.

Greek wine law

As well as the Traditional Appellation granted to Retsina, the rest of the Greek wine law is modelled on the French system. 'Appellation of Superior Quality' is the quality wine designation covering dry wines, whilst 'Controlled Appellation of Origin' covers the quality sweet wines. There is also an equivalent of Vin de Pays (actually often using the French description on the label).

The wine regions of Greece

Macedonia is best known for its red wines. Important regions include Naoussa, Goumenissa and the Côtes de Meliton. The latter is the appellation covering Greece's most famous wine estate, Château Carras. Zitsa, a crisp white wine, is the best known wine from Epirus. The

Retsina ancient and modern

Thoughts of the Classical World are unlikely to be present when the average tourist has their first run-in with Retsina. This resinated dry white wine is still available throughout Greece and on many export markets. It is made by adding Aleppo pine

Peloponnese has some important wine districts. Mantinia produces some fresh dry white wines. Nemea is renowned for its reds. Mavrodaphne of Patras is a sweet fortified red wine like Port.

Of the Ionian Islands, Cephalonia has the best reputation for its wines. In the Cyclades, Santorini makes some good dry whites (and a delicious Vin Santo, *see page 124*) and Paros some decent reds. The island of Samos specialises in a range of lusciously sweet white wines made from Muscat. Crete's main vineyard areas, such as Peza, lie south of Heraklion.

CYPRUS

Like all the Mediterranean countries, Cyprus has a history of wine production going back to Ancient times. More recently the island's grape growers and winemakers have had to contend with big changes in the market for their products. A generation ago a lot of cheap bulk wine was sold to Eastern Europe. This market has declined, so the wine industry is working to improve the quality of its light wines.

Cyprus has managed to stay *Phylloxera* free. The main native black grape is the Mavro. Xynisteri is the principal indigenous white grape. There are vineyards planted all the way from sea level right up into the Troodos mountains.

The island's most distinctive wine is Commandaria. It is produced from grapes that have been raisined in the sun. A partial fermentation takes place, before the addition of grape spirit and maturation in wood. The resulting wine is dark in colour, with a heavy, raisiny nose and palate.

THE EASTERN MEDITERRANEAN

Although Turkey is a massive grape grower, the majority of this fruit is for table use or raisining. The wines that are produced tend to be very ordinary.

Lebanon produces the most impressive wines in the Middle East. Châteaux Musar and Kefraya make full-bodied reds using Cabernet Sauvignon and other black grapes of French origin.

Israel makes some decent wines, particularly from grapes grown in the cooler mountainous vineyards of Galilee.

Egypt is responsible for producing some very basic wine from vineyards near Alexandria.

NORTH AFRICA

Algeria was an enormous wine producer during the French colonial period. The folklore is that Algerian wine was always used to beef up the lesser red Burgundies. Ever since independence in 1962 the Algerian wine industry has been in decline. The area under vine is one-sixth of what it was before the Second World War, with a large proportion of the grapes now being grown for table use. The hot climate tends to favour the production of reds and rosés. Traditionally, Algeria has been mainly planted with the same sort of varieties as Languedoc-Roussillon: Carignan, Alicante Bouschet, Cinsault and Grenache.

Morocco has also seen its wine industry contract following independence.

Tunisia follows the pattern of its western neighbours in seeing a contraction of vineyard area over the last 50 years. As well as reds, white wines from the Muscat grape are produced.

The boom in New World wine sales in Britain over the last 15 years has changed the wine market forever. All the significant New World wine producing countries have clocked up awesome rates of growth, with Australia in the van. In fact, Australia is now the second most important wine supplier to the UK market, and there is talk of France's pre-eminence coming under threat.

Several factors seem to have been responsible for the extraordinary success of the New World wines. Firstly, most wineries in the New World are capable of making clean, consistent, reliable wines

The New World

year in year out. This has made buying a Chilean, Californian or Australian wine pretty much a safe bet. A related factor is the general style of New World wines, which tend to be characterised by a big blast of ripe fruit, often backed up by a sizeable thwack of oak. Whilst such wines arguably lack subtlety, their showiness and brute force appeal to many of today's wine drinkers.

The no-nonsense presentation of most New World wines has doubtless helped the cause. The use of varietal labelling has taken much of the terror out of buying wine. Remembering the names of a couple of favourite grape varieties allows wine drinkers to get by without recourse to a degree in modern languages. Many New World wine producers have also been fervent users of back labels to convey consumer-friendly information, such as service temperatures and suggested food partnerships.

Another factor where the New World scores is in delivering good wine at a sensible price. Punters have realised that while the average New World wine may be a bit more expensive than its Old World competitor, it is more likely to provide satisfaction.

● wine producing town or village
◯ other wine producing area

North America

The USA is the fourth largest wine producer in the world. With over 90% of that wine being produced in the state of California, to some extent the story of American wine is the story of Californian wine. However, Canada with its Ice Wines, Oregon with its Pinot Noirs and many of Washington State's red wines merit attention from the globe-trotting wine drinker.

Despite the struggles of the pioneers, by the beginning of the twentieth century the American wine industry was going through its first Golden Age. California had built up a strong market for its wines not just in the USA, but in export markets. Disaster came in the form of National Prohibition. The Americans convinced themselves that many of society's evils were the result of booze, and that by banning alcohol the world would become a better place. The US Constitution was amended in 1919 to bring in Prohibition. It is well documented that as a piece of social engineering Prohibition was a disaster. However, the fledgling wine industry was devastated. Those vineyards that did survive were dedicated to producing grapes for home winemaking.

Prohibition was repealed in 1933. The wine industry was slow to recover. Much of the wine produced in the USA until the 1960s was fortified and sweet. Since then many parts of the USA have come to realise that the potential exists for serious wine production.

Whilst there is nothing in the USA equivalent to Appellation Contrôlée, there is a scheme that allows the mapping out and naming of defined regions. The system of 'American Viticultural Areas' (AVAs) guarantees that a wine comes from where it says it does. Beyond that there are no rules about varieties to be planted, yields etc., as there are in EU quality wine regimes.

PACIFIC NORTH-WEST

Washington State and Oregon have developed their wine industries since the Second World War.

Most of Washington's vineyards lie inland from Seattle, over the Cascade Ranges. This results in

The world of wine

an extreme continental climate, with bitterly cold winters and hot summers. Rainfall is negligible, so irrigation is necessary. The Columbia Valley AVA encompasses two other AVAs, Yakima Valley and Walla Walla Valley. Merlot is Washington's flagship grape, but some very good wines have also been made from Syrah and Cabernet Sauvignon.

The vineyards in Oregon lie much closer to the Pacific Ocean than their neighbours in Washington State. This gives Oregon's vineyards a distinctly cool climate feel. The key Willamette Valley AVA lies in between Portland and Eugene. The growers in Oregon have taken the decidedly risky option of focusing their fledgling industry on the Pinot Noir. Some good wines have been made, but working with Pinot Noir in a marginal climate is always going to be a roller-coaster ride.

NORTH-EASTERN USA

Because so little of it is exported, it is easy to underestimate how much grape growing goes on east of the Rockies. New York State is the most famous East Coast wine producer. The limiting factor on the East Coast of the USA is the severity of the winters. To cope with this, in the past many of the vines planted in New York State were hybrids of the American vine species, *Vitis labrusca*. These hybrid vines (such as Catawba and Concord) can survive cold winters, but the flavour of the wines produced from *Vitis labrusca* grapes disagrees with drinkers who were raised on *Vitis vinifera* wine. A number of wineries are now working with French hybrid varieties (like Seyval Blanc) and normal *Vitis vinifera* varieties (such as Chardonnay and Riesling). AVAs in New

York State include the Finger Lakes and the Hudson River Region. There are even some vineyards at the eastern end of Long Island.

There are isolated vineyards all the way from Massachusetts down to Virginia and beyond.

CANADA

Canada still has a relatively small wine industry, although it is growing very quickly. The limiting factor – the severe winters – is the same as in the north-eastern states of the USA. Like New York State, *Vitis labrusca* vines and French hybrids dominated the industry until fairly recently. This is now changing, with increasing plantings of *Vitis vinifera* vines. The climate favours white wine production, although some decent reds are being made. Canada's one outstanding speciality is Ice Wine. This is made from frozen grapes in the same way as its German and Austrian cousins.

The two main vineyard areas of Canada are the Niagara Peninsula in Ontario and the Okanagan Valley in British Columbia. The climate of both areas benefits from the moderating effect of the nearby lakes. The quality wine seal for Canada is administered by the Vintners' Quality Alliance (VQA).

MEXICO

Although Mexico has a significant amount of land under vine, the production of bottled wine is not that large. A lot of the grapes are for table use or raisining, and much of the wine is distilled to make brandy. Some reasonable red wines are made, with the Petite Sirah and Cabernet Sauvignon being two of the varieties grown.

Far right: Vineyards in the Okanagan Valley of British Columbia.

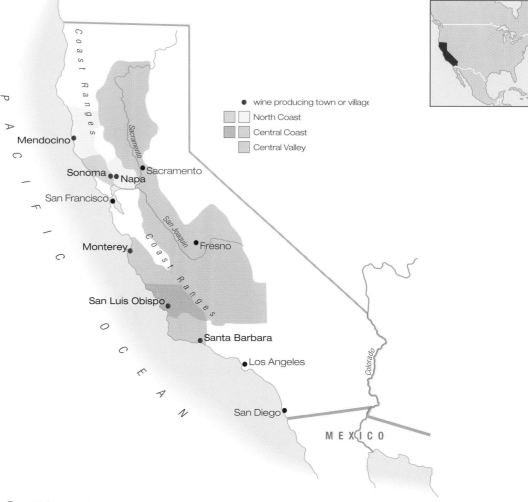

California

Earthquakes are probably the least of the hazards that the grape grower and winemaker in California have had to face over the last century. The industry has had to cope with everything from dodgy rootstocks to dodgy legislation. In spite of these challenges, California has become a thriving and confident wine producer.

California's first wines were produced by Spanish missionaries, who were gradually working their way up the west coast of North America at the end of the eighteenth century. Commercial wine production started during the first half of the nineteenth century, and was greatly boosted by the Gold Rush and the opening of the transcontinental railroad. Despite the first appearance of *Phylloxera* in California in the 1870s and the resulting need to replant on rootstocks, the wine industry was making progress. Prohibition, two World Wars and the Depression pushed things back during the first half of the twentieth century. However, since then an innovative and vibrant wine industry has emerged. Some of the world's most important grape and wine research has been carried out at the University of California at Davis and at Fresno State University.

Even so, the wine industry has not been without its worries. The recommended rootstock in California until the 1980s was called AxR-1. It flourished in the fertile soils of California and gave a big crop. Then, about 20 years ago, growers began to notice some of their vines were starting to die. Investigations revealed that a strain of *Phylloxera* named 'Biotype B' was happily munching its way through the AxR-1 rootstocks. This has meant that through the 1990s many of California's existing vineyards have had to be grubbed up and replanted with properly resistant rootstocks.

The vineyard regions

Given the latitude of California (34°North runs through Los Angeles), most parts of the state are going to have a hot climate. This is certainly true

of California's largest vineyard region, the Central Valley. Cut off from the Pacific Ocean by the Coast Ranges, the sweltering Central Valley churns out California's basic wines (sometimes referred to as 'jug wines'). In fact, a lot of the vines grown in the Central Valley (varieties like Thompson Seedless) are there for table grape and raisin production, rather than winemaking.

The key to premium wine production in California is proximity to the Pacific Ocean. The California Current brings cold water down the west coast of North America. The breezes and fogs generated by the cold ocean water temper the climate of California's coastal vineyards.

The most famous vineyard areas to enjoy the moderating effect of the Pacific Ocean lie directly north of San Francisco. Napa, Sonoma and

The Santa Maria Valley produces some of California's most elegant and subtle wines.

Mendocino counties (sometimes lumped together as 'North Coast') between them produce the vast majority of California's great wines. The Napa Valley, though not large in volume terms, is the emotional heart of California's wine industry.

AVAs

A number of small AVAs have been defined within these famous counties: in the Napa – Rutherford, Oakville, Stags Leap, Mount Veeder, Howell Mountain, Atlas Peak; in Sonoma – Sonoma Valley, Alexander Valley, Dry Creek Valley, Russian River Valley; in Mendocino – Anderson Valley.

The premium cool climate Carneros AVA, which lies close to San Pablo Bay, is shared between Napa and Sonoma counties.

Astronomical land prices in the Napa Valley in particular have encouraged many wineries to search elsewhere in California for premium-quality fruit. The main focus of attention has been the Central Coast, which runs from San Francisco south to virtually within striking distance of Los Angeles. Just as in the North Coast regions, the Pacific Ocean is a moderating influence on the climate of the Central Coast, as is altitude in some circumstances. The principal wine producing counties are Monterey, San Luis Obispo and Santa Barbara. Individual important AVAs include Santa Cruz Mountains, Paso Robles, Santa Maria Valley and Santa Ynez Valley.

Grapes and wines

With the exception of Zinfandel and Petite Sirah, the black grape varieties grown in California are a fairly familiar line-up. Risking the odd death threat from Australia, it is fair to say that outside Bordeaux the Californians produce more fine Cabernet Sauvignon than anyone else. The top Californian Merlots can be pretty impressive, too. Quite a number of super-premium 'Bordeaux Blends' (Cabernet Sauvignon and Merlot, plus the occasional dash of Cabernet Franc, Malbec and Petit Verdot) are also on the market (sometimes referred to as 'Meritage' wines in the USA). The Napa Valley remains the finest area for these Bordeaux-inspired reds, although the Alexander Valley and the Santa Cruz Mountains are also responsible for some great Cabernets. The fickle Pinot Noir has been successfully planted in a number of California's coolest AVAs: Carneros, Russian River Valley and Santa Maria Valley. Given California's 'Mediterranean' climate, it is strange that it has taken until relatively recently for the industry to lock on to Syrah and Sangiovese.

However, for many wine drinkers California will always be inexorably associated with Zinfandel. The best of these are often made from ancient vines that were planted before Prohibition (Sonoma County seems to have best preserved its heritage of old vines). Rich, dark and mouth-filling, a top Zinfandel can stop you in your tracks. The irony is that until its recently acquired cult status, many growers were at a loss as to what to do with their Zinfandel grapes. Hence the idea of vinifying the Zinfandel as a medium rosé, with the resulting invention of 'White Zinfandel' or 'Blush'. For the cognoscenti, other surviving pre-*Phylloxera* varieties like Petite Sirah (probably not 'real' Syrah) and Mataro (Mourvèdre) also make some fascinating red wines.

Best Buy

Geyser Peak Sauvignon Blanc 2000

Pale lemon. Light, fresh and crisp. There are touches of apple on the nose, with a hint of melon as well. Dry, mid-acidity, mid-high alcohol. Lightish-bodied. There is an attractive zesty zing on the mid-palate. Green fruit. Mid-length.

Being facetious, the Californian for white wine is Chardonnay. Although fine, elegant, subtle Chardonnays are made in California, a lot of them are oaky, off-dry and confected. Many of the best Chardonnays come from the same sort of cool areas that grow the Pinot Noir. Even in its oak-aged Fumé Blanc guise, Sauvignon Blanc doesn't seem to do it for most American drinkers. With declining interest in varieties like Riesling and Chenin Blanc as well, about ten years ago the nightmare that soon Chardonnay would be the only white variety grown west of the Rockies looked like coming true. Then the Californians discovered Viognier. Rich and opulent, with low acid-ity and high alcohol, most important of all Viognier is reasonably compatible with oak (mandatory for success on the US market). The first rash of Californian Viogniers have included some attrac-tive wines, so if nothing else you will have some-thing to drink in California if you develop an allergy to Chardonnay. If you develop an allergy to oak, you'll just die.

Attractive traditional method sparkling wines are produced in California. Several of the big Champagne companies have subsidiaries here and, wanting to protect the kudos of their Cham-pagnes, they often market their Californian sparkl-ing wines at prices well below their Champagnes.

Best Buy

St. Francis Sonoma County Old Vine Zinfandel 1998

Deepish ruby core. Mid-ruby rim. Spicy, heady and juicy on the nose. Strawberry jam and liquorice. Super ripe. Dry, low acidity, very warm alcohol. Full-bodied (verging on massive) and succulent. Sweet oak comes through. The tannins are submerged under the fleshy richness. Long, peppery finish.

Vineyard and water tower at St. Helena in the Napa Valley, California's most famous vineyard area.

The world of wine

South America

If a man rushes up to you in the street and asks you which wine producing area he should invest in, tell him South America. The raw potential of Chile and Argentina remains superb. Chile has a head start, but Argentina is now beginning to make its move in the world wine stakes.

CHILE

Chile is the South American country that has led the way in building a high-quality, export-orientated wine industry. This in spite of the fact that Argentina is a much bigger producer, and that Chile only 20 years ago was primarily producing basic wines for its home market. It seems to have taken until the 1980s for winemakers and investors to realise the potential of Chile as a premium wine producer. Since then investment in Chile's wine industry has been enormous, and the results are impressive to taste. What is more, most Chilean wine is still easy on the pocket.

Chile's greatest asset is its viticulture. Firstly, it is one of the few places in the world that is free of *Phylloxera*. Therefore vine growers do not have to graft their vines. Secondly, because of the dryness of the climate there is only the occasional outbreak of fungal disease. The biggest worry in vineyard regions that are warm and dry like Chile is lack of water. This is where Chile's proximity to the Andes mountains provides a third crucial advantage. Most winters bring a heavy snowfall to the mountains. As this snow melts in the spring and summer it provides a source of irrigation water exactly when the vines need it. A fourth important element is that labour costs are still relatively low.

When the Chilean export boom started, many of the wines were decent, but it was obvious that the winemaking equipment and expertise still trailed some way behind the likes of California and Australia. The massive investment of recent years in hardware and expertise has addressed these shortcomings. Today Chile has some of the best-equipped and operated wineries in the world.

Varietals

The varietal line-up is pretty familiar, with Chardonnay and Sauvignon Blanc the key white grapes, and Cabernet Sauvignon and Merlot the main black grapes. Other black varieties like Pinot Noir, Syrah and Sangiovese have also been planted successfully. The traditional black grape variety of Chile was the Pais, but this is rarely if ever exported. One of the more bizarre aspects of the Chilean vineyards was the discovery that not everything that had been planted as Sauvignon Blanc or Merlot was what it claimed to be. Much of the Sauvignon Blanc turned out to be a less aromatic variety called Sauvignonasse. Care is now taken to ensure that new plantings are the genuine Sauvignon Blanc. The problem with Merlot has unpredictably turned into a huge marketing success. Many of the older 'Merlot' vineyards are planted with a mixture of 'real' Merlot and another black variety called Carmenère. Carmenère, like Merlot and Cabernet Sauvignon, originated in Bordeaux, although nowadays it is virtually extinct on its home patch. With its deep colour, intense herbal and red pepper aromas, and juicy lushness on the palate, it has been adopted by Chile as its own 'unique' vine.

Wine districts

Running from north to south, Chile's main wine districts are: Aconcagua Valley, Maipo Valley, Rapel Valley, Curicó Valley and Maule Valley. All of these areas lie some distance inland from the Pacific Ocean, with the coastal mountain range cutting out much of the maritime influence. However, in recent years there has been a lot of

Best Buy

Errazuriz Aconcagua Cabernet Sauvignon Reserva, Don Maximiano Estate 1998

Opaque, blackish purple core. Narrow pink-purple rim. On the nose, there is an immediate attack of dark fruit, blackcurrant in particular. Plenty of smoky, toasty oak follows through as well. Dry, low acidity, high alcohol. Intensely lush and full-bodied. The fruit is underpinned by some ripe tannins. Long finish. Like many New World Cabernets, this wine is approachable despite its extreme youth. However, it will keep for at least five years and with time may well become more rounded and complex. (Just thinking about quaffing this wine with fillet steak is making me drool.)

interest in a new district called the Casablanca Valley. This area lies quite close to the Pacific Ocean, so its climate is much cooler than the more traditional inland areas. Not surprisingly Casablanca is producing some of Chile's most impressive white wines.

ARGENTINA

Argentina has long been South America's sleeping giant when it comes to wine. The country is the fifth largest wine producer in the world. Yet until recently very little Argentinian wine was seen on the export market. This was not surprising as

Geared up for export demand. The Caliterra winery in Chile's Rapel Valley.

much of the Argentinian wine produced in the past was pretty basic stuff for the home market.

The picture has started to change for the better. At last Argentina is going through a period when it is both politically and economically reasonably stable. A number of wineries have started to focus on quality wines for the export market. Investment from overseas has helped, as has a band of 'flying winemakers'. The term 'flying winemaker' is used to describe a winemaker (often Australian) who helps a winery, on a contract basis, to produce wines in a modern style that will work on the export market.

The potential for quality wine production in Argentina is very high. The vineyard regions share a similar climate to Chile, with conditions overall being warm and dry. The Andes are on hand to provide irrigation water. There is *Phylloxera* in Argentina, but its spread has been slow. Vineyard yields in some cases are mind bogglingly high. One element of the move to better quality has been convincing growers that they need to rein back the volume a bit.

Varietal line-up

Argentina has an eclectic grape variety line-up, determined until recently by where each wave of European immigrants came from. The Criolla and Cereza grape varieties are important for commodity wine production in Argentina (in the same way that the Pais is in Chile). Although varieties like Chenin Blanc, Chardonnay and Viognier are planted, some of the country's most distinctive dry white wines are made from a grape variety called the Torrontés (originally from northern Spain).

Torrontés produces wines with an intense floral aroma (a bit like Muscat) and a light freshness on the palate. Amongst the black grapes, as well as varieties like Cabernet Sauvignon and Syrah, there are sizeable plantings of Tempranillo and Bonarda (originally from Piemonte in Italy). However, the variety that has become Argentina's flagship abroad is the Malbec. There are smatterings of Malbec in Bordeaux, and it is the key grape used to make Cahors. But in Argentina it has proved a big success. A good Argentinian Malbec has a deep colour, plenty of robust dark fruit, followed by a full-bodied, but not particularly tannic, palate.

By far the largest wine region in Argentina is Mendoza. The other significant region, San Juan, lies a little way further north.

URUGUAY

Uruguay has a relatively small wine industry. Most of what is produced there is drunk on the home market. The country's most distinctive wines are mid-bodied reds made from the Tannat grape. This variety was brought to Uruguay at the end of the nineteenth century by settlers from southwestern France.

BRAZIL

Brazil is the third largest wine producer in South America after Argentina and Chile. Most of the vineyards are in the extreme south of the country in the state of Rio Grande do Sul. Even here the climate is sub-tropical, and this will always pose problems of ripeness and fungal disease. Most of the wines are of simple quality.

Best Buy

Malbec 'Oak Cask', Mendoza, Trapiche 1997

Dark ruby core. Narrowish pink rim. A chunky aroma of damsons and oak. Some spicy, inky notes as well. Dry, low acidity, high alcohol. Pretty full-bodied. Fleshy, supple tannins. Impressively ripe fruit. Mid-length. Drinking well now, but will keep for three to five years.

169

South America

The world of wine

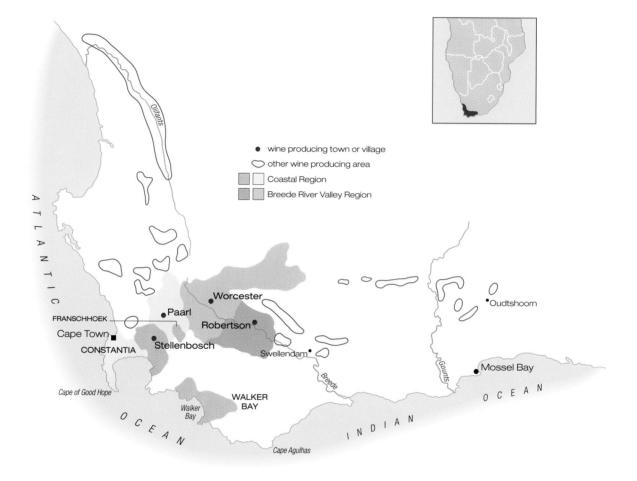

- ● wine producing town or village
- ◯ other wine producing area
- ▢ Coastal Region
- ▢ Breede River Valley Region

Olifants

ATLANTIC

Worcester

Paarl

FRANSCHHOEK

Cape Town

Robertson

CONSTANTIA

Stellenbosch

Swellendam

Oudtshoorn

Breede

Gourits

Mossel Bay

Cape of Good Hope

Walker Bay

WALKER BAY

OCEAN

INDIAN

OCEAN

Cape Agulhas

South Africa

The South African wine industry, like the country as a whole, is in a state of flux. There is still a lot of restructuring going on following the end of apartheid. The optimists see a rather rosy future for South African wine. Certainly exports to key markets such as the UK continue to flourish.

The first vineyards in southern Africa were planted by the Dutch in the seventeenth century (the first vintage was 1659). Since then the South African wine industry has gone through several cycles of boom and bust. It will be interesting to see how the industry adapts to life in the new South Africa, with a lot depending on the economic and political stability of the country in the years to come.

The Dutch realised that the climate in most of southern Africa is far too hot for wine production. It is really only in the region immediately around Cape Town that the cooling effect of the Atlantic Ocean makes grape growing realistic. The heat and dryness even here though is reflected in the bush fires that have caused extensive vineyard damage in recent years.

Dramatic granite mountains tower over the Boschendal estate in Franschhoek.

The world of wine

White varietals

The varietal composition of South Africa's vineyards is a bit different from the standard New World template. The most widely planted white grape is the Chenin Blanc (known locally as the 'Steen'). This variety alone makes up a third of South Africa's total vineyard area. In South Africa, Chenin Blanc produces light, clean, simple dry white wines. They are generally very inexpensive. A number of growers are striving to make something a bit more characterful, working with old vines and in some cases oak barrels. For premium white wines the Chardonnay and Sauvignon Blanc are preferred. The Cape produces some very impressive Chardonnays, both in the oaked style and in the newly fashionable 'unwooded'

style. Sauvignon Blanc has been more of a struggle, not least because a lot of it was originally planted in areas that were too warm. Where Sauvignon Blanc has been planted on cooler sites, and then carefully vinified, some attractive wines have been produced.

Black varietals

On the black grape front, South Africa is again a bit different from the rest of the New World. Pinotage is South Africa's baby, having been developed at Stellenbosch in the 1920s. It was for a long time rather looked down upon in South Africa. However, with the end of apartheid demand on the export markets skyrocketed, creating a shortage of Pinotage and forcing the price up. Much Pinotage is harmless, glugging red wine. However, some of the estates with 'old' Pinotage vines make a more serious wine that can age. Given the relative scarcity of Pinotage, a lot of South Africa's cheaper reds are made from Cinsaut (the Cinsault of the southern Rhône) and/or Ruby Cabernet (a cross of Cabernet Sauvignon and Carignan).

Shiraz should be able to produce great wines in the Cape, given the warm climate and the granite soils. Progress was held back by the high incidence of viral disease in much of the Shiraz planted in South Africa. This problem is now being tackled and some very good Shiraz wines are emerging. Cabernet Sauvignon (and Cabernet-based blends) remains the mainstay of the premium red wine sector. Old style examples were often earthy and stringy, but a couple of dozen estates now make classy Cabernets that can

An aerial view of Franschhoek.

stand comparison with equivalent wines from elsewhere in the New World.

Co-operative wineries and new technology

Another of South Africa's quirks when compared with the rest of the New World was the actual structure of the wine industry. In Australia or California most wineries either own their vineyards, or buy in grapes from private farmers. South Africa used to be set up much more like parts of southern Europe, where most of the winemaking is done by co-operative wineries. In other words, individual growers deliver their grapes to a jointly owned co-operative winery. The winery makes the wine, sells it and then pays the growers a dividend based on the quantity (and hopefully the quality) of the fruit that was delivered. The biggest co-operative in South Africa used to be the KWV (the Cape Winegrowers Co-operative). As well as being the country's biggest wine producer, in the old days the KWV actually had regulatory control over many aspects of the wine industry. This rather sinister monolith has been dismantled, and the winemaking side functions much more like a normal (large-scale) wine producer.

There was a time after the Second World War when the South African industry probably led the world in its use of technology in the winery (such as the temperature control of fermentation). The growing isolation of the apartheid period led to the country falling behind the rapid progress being made in the outside world. However, the last few years have seen a lot of investment aimed at catching up with the competition.

Wine producing regions

South Africa has a system for legally defining the origin of its wines. 'Wine of Origin' (WO) is not as prescriptive as Appellation Contrôlée. However, it does mean that if a consumer buys something that says 'Stellenbosch Pinotage 2001' on the label then that is what will be in the bottle.

All of South Africa's significant vineyard areas are within 150 km (93 miles) of Cape Town. WO Constantia is South Africa's oldest wine region and lies just outside the city. Elinor in Jane Austen's *Sense and Sensibility* consoles herself with a glass of finest old Constantia. WO Stellenbosch is also relatively cool and probably makes more top-flight wines than any other part of South Africa. A little way further inland is WO Paarl, another area capable of making some very good wines. The sub-district, WO Franschhoek, is particularly highly regarded. These areas are often grouped together and sold under the Wine of Origin 'Coastal Region'.

One further hop inland brings you to the hot, irrigated areas of WO Worcester and WO Robertson. These areas produce inexpensive white wines, fortified wines and brandy.

Lying south of all these districts and facing the Atlantic Ocean is WO Walker Bay. With its cool climate this area makes fine Chardonnays and world-class Pinot Noir.

ZIMBABWE

This country has a small wine industry that has occasionally exported in the past. The tropical climate will probably prevent Zimbabwe from ever being anything more than a niche player.

Louisvale Stellenbosch Chardonnay 1996

Bright, mid-gold appearance. Intense and opulent on the nose, with a warm richness to the fore. Peach and mango. Some buttery notes as well. Dry, mid-low acidity, high alcohol. Mid-full bodied. Open-textured fruitiness. The spiciness of the oak comes through on the mid-palate. Very harmonious. Long finish.

Bellingham Coastal Region Pinotage 1999

Moderately deep pink-ruby core. Mid-pink rim. A fairly intense aroma, with plenty of upfront jammy fruit and some spicy notes. Quite a distinctive 'coal dust' edge as well. Dry, low acidity, high alcohol. Mid-full bodied. Softish tannins. Broad and open textured. Soft, ripe fruit. Mid-length.

Australia

The awesome success of the Australian wine industry over the last 15 years has been one of the defining features of today's global wine market. In that time Australian wine has gone from being a fascinating niche product, to capturing significant market share not only in the UK but also in Scandinavia, North America and Asia.

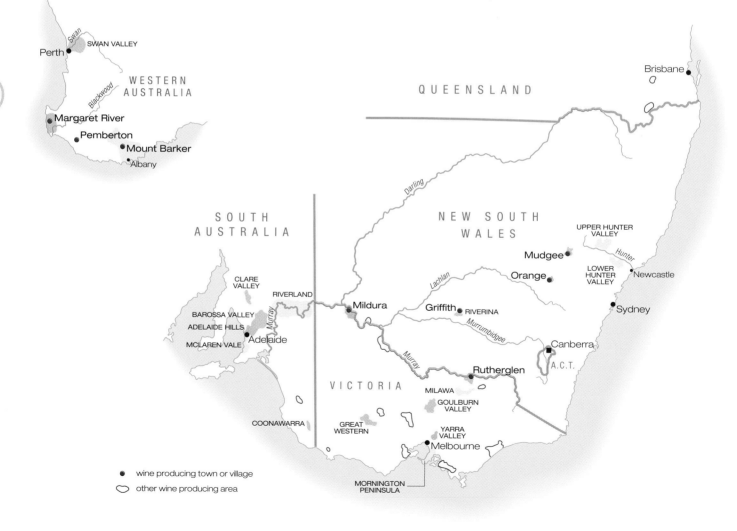

Perth
SWAN VALLEY
Swan
WESTERN AUSTRALIA
Blackwood
Margaret River
Pemberton
Mount Barker
Albany

Brisbane
QUEENSLAND

Darling

SOUTH AUSTRALIA
NEW SOUTH WALES
UPPER HUNTER VALLEY
Mudgee
Hunter
Orange
LOWER HUNTER VALLEY
Newcastle
CLARE VALLEY
Lachlan
RIVERLAND
Mildura
Griffith
RIVERINA
Sydney
BAROSSA VALLEY
Murrumbidgee
ADELAIDE HILLS
Murray
MCLAREN VALE
Adelaide
Canberra
A.C.T.
Rutherglen
VICTORIA
MILAWA
Murray
GOULBURN VALLEY
COONAWARRA
GREAT WESTERN
YARRA VALLEY
Melbourne

● wine producing town or village
⬭ other wine producing area

MORNINGTON PENINSULA

Given Australia's export successes, it would surprise many people to know that in crude volume terms the country is still not a massive wine producer. However, new vineyards are being planted all the time and every week seems to see a new winery opening its gates.

The first vineyards were planted in Australia a couple of hundred years ago. Not much became of those initial efforts, probably because the vines were planted in the wrong sort of sites. It was a Scotsman called James Busby who many would say got things off to a proper start. Busby took a selection of vine cuttings out to Australia in the 1830s, and demonstrated that vines could flourish in the Hunter Valley. Bit by bit Australia's other classic vineyard regions came to be planted during the nineteenth century. Between the First and Second World Wars there was a boom in exports to the UK, but most of what was being sold was pretty basic fortified wine. It was only in the 1950s that a new generation of winemakers, most notably Max Schubert at Penfolds, started to demonstrate that Australia could be a producer of some impressive light wines. Since then the momentum has slowly built up, and Australia is now poised to become one of the key players in a world wine market increasingly dominated by powerful brands.

White varietals

As well as the inevitable Chardonnay, Australia's two other leading white varieties are Sémillon and Riesling. These days a lot of Sémillon ends up disappearing into blends with Chardonnay or other less thrilling partners. In many ways this is a shame, as Sémillon can produce some fascinating dry white wines. One surviving tradition in Australia is to bottle Sémillon young, with no oak ageing, and then leave the wine to age for ten years or more. What emerges after this extended bottle maturation is a wine with extraordinary smoky and nutty complexity. Riesling struggles commercially in Australia, as it does in the rest of the English-speaking world. However, some of the country's most beautiful and elegant white wines are Rieslings. The best examples tend to be produced in a dry or off-dry style, with a good concentration of limey fruit when young, which with bottle age rapidly develops a powerful diesel oil and 'gas pipe' bouquet (these are excellent to drink – despite my description).

There has long been a tradition in parts of Australia of growing the Verdelho grape. This variety is best known as one of the grapes used to make Madeira. However, the current revival of interest in Verdelho involves using it to make dry white wines with a distinctive ripe green fruit character. Marsanne is another stalwart variety in some of Victoria's vineyards.

Black varietals

Shiraz and Cabernet Sauvignon are the leading black grape varieties. With these two big hitters around it is understandable that it has taken some time for Merlot to establish itself in Australia. Given the heat in many regions of Australia, Pinot Noir would not be a first-choice variety. That said, some small-scale wineries in the cooler districts of Victoria, Tasmania and Western Australia have made some delicious Pinots. Perhaps the most interesting varietal development of recent years has been the emergence of Grenache and Mourvèdre from the shadows. These two varieties have been planted in Australia since the nineteenth century, but most of the wine made from them has ended up in anonymous blends or in 'Australian Port'. A number of juicy, jammy, decadently alcoholic straight Grenaches are now available from the Barossa and Clare Valleys. Even more impressive are the rash of 'Southern Rhône type' blends, combining Grenache, Mourvèdre and Shiraz.

Wine producing regions

The northern half of Australia is far too hot for grape growing, so it is best left to uranium mines and crocodiles. Around 97% of Australia's vineyards are planted in the south-eastern corner of the country. As well as enjoying a more moderate climate, this is the most densely populated part of Australia, so the initial vineyards were very close to their potential markets. Although it is possible to dry-farm vines in some parts of Australia, virtually all newly planted sites are rigged up with irrigation drippers.

Rosemount's Roxburgh Vineyard in the Hunter Valley, responsible for one of Australia's finest Chardonnays.

NEW SOUTH WALES

The most famous vineyard region in New South Wales is the Hunter Valley. Although many of Australia's principal grape varieties are grown there, it is best known for its Sémillon and Shiraz. The Hunter Valley is hot and humid, so not surprisingly wine producers have looked elsewhere for cooler and drier sites. Mudgee lies inland from the Hunter Valley and is now making impressive red wines. At an altitude of 1000 m (3281 ft), the Orange vineyards are some of the highest in the world. Look out for Orange Chardonnays, which have finesse and good balancing acidity. Inland, close to the town of Griffith, are the irrigated vineyards near the River Murrumbidgee. This region nowadays calls itself 'Riverina'. Although it makes some fine sweet wines, Riverina is primarily a producer of inexpensive bulk wines and its volume output makes New South Wales the second largest wine producing state in Australia.

VICTORIA

The Yarra Valley just outside Melbourne is Victoria's leading cool climate vineyard region, with a reputation for its Pinot Noir and Chardonnay. The nearby Mornington Peninsula also makes some impressive wines. Venturing inland the climate gets warmer, with the Great Western Region best known for its sparkling wines. As well as conventional white and rosé sparkling wines, it is worth mentioning Australia's pride and joy, Sparkling Shiraz. Made by the traditional method, these red wines are amongst the richest and fruitiest sparkling wines in the world. Also lying inland, but focusing on light wine production are the

Goulburn Valley and Milawa. In the hot interior of Victoria, close to the Murray River, is the town of Rutherglen. The wineries here produce Australia's great fortified sweet white wines. The grapes used are Muscat and Muscadelle (called 'Tokay' in Australia). The best examples receive long maturation in wood, resulting in a deep amber brown colour and a rich, raisiny character on the nose and palate. Victoria has its own large-volume, irrigated production area down the River Murray at Mildura. Victoria is the third largest wine producing state in Australia.

TASMANIA

Lying south of mainland Australia and surrounded by the ocean, Tasmania has a distinctly cool grape growing climate. Not surprisingly, Pinot Noir is the favoured variety.

SOUTH AUSTRALIA

South Australia is the quality and quantity powerhouse of the Australian wine industry. It is responsible for producing half of the country's wine and is the home base for most of Australia's large wine companies.

The Riverland is the big-volume region lying inland along the River Murray. Although rarely named on the label, a good proportion of the liquid in bottles of inexpensive branded Australian wine will have come from the Riverland. Just north of Adelaide is South Australia's most famous wine district, the Barossa Valley. Many would say that this is the origin of Australia's definitive Shiraz wines. The Barossa also produces some very good Rieslings. A little further north is the Clare

Brown Brothers King Valley Riesling 2000

Pale lemon. Fragrant and lifted. Lime chunks. Just starting to develop some petrol / diesel notes. Very refined. Dryish, mid-acidity, moderate alcohol. Mid-bodied. Clean and elegant. Mid-length.

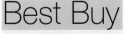

Rosemount McClaren Vale 'GSM' (Grenache / Shiraz / Mourvèdre) 1998

Deep purple core. Narrow pink rim. A big attack of super-ripe dark fruits. Bramble, blueberry and prune. Rich, juicy and spicy. Dry, low acidity, very high alcohol. Full-bodied and lush. Spicy and fruity on the mid-palate. Supple, rounded tannins. Long finish.

Above: It's that Hill of Grace vineyard again. Located just above the Barossa Valley, the vineyard takes its name from the neighbouring Gnadenberg church.
Far right: Vineyards in the Hawkes Bay region of New Zealand.

South Australia is blessed with being *Phylloxera* free. As well as not having to graft, one aspect of South Australia is that some of the vines planted there in the nineteenth century are still alive and productive (*see page 36*).

WESTERN AUSTRALIA

Although still small in volume terms, many commentators claim that Western Australia produces some of the country's top-quality wines. The state's historic vineyard region is the Swan Valley, just upriver from Perth. However, the extremely high temperatures experienced in the Swan sent people south in search of cooler climate areas. The Margaret River is now well established as one of Australia's premium wine districts, producing impressive reds and whites. The vineyards in Pemberton and Mount Barker are also crafting some stylish wines.

Valley, another area renowned for its Rieslings. Directly to the east of the city of Adelaide is the cool Adelaide Hills area, where some stylish reds and whites are produced. A short distance south of Adelaide is another of South Australia's classic wine regions, McClaren Vale. It can rival the Barossa with the quality of the best of its Shiraz wines. At the southernmost extremity of the state is the region of Coonawarra. Despite possessing a motel called the Chardonnay Lodge, Coonawarra is Australia's best region for Cabernet Sauvignon. The climate is cool and maritime. This, and the distinctive red loam soil called 'terra rossa', seem to be ideal for Cabernet.

The role of the winemakers

Whilst the climate and other viticultural factors, as well as some shrewd marketing, have contributed to the success of Australian wine, the massive input made by Australia's winemakers should not be underestimated. It is their skill and perseverance that have made Australia's wines some of the cleanest, fruitiest and most reliable in the world. The fact that the Australian industry is comparatively lightly regulated has helped by allowing a great deal of experimentation and innovation. Many of Australia's leading winemakers studied at Roseworthy College in South Australia. It says a lot for Roseworthy that its alumni now make wine in almost every grape growing country on earth.

The world of wine

● wine producing town or village

Auckland

North
Island

Gisborne
Poverty Bay

HAWKES BAY
Napier
Hastings
Hawke
Bay

Wellington

Nelson
Blenheim   MARTINBOROUGH
MARLBOROUGH

CANTERBURY
Christchurch

South
Island

OTAGO

Dunedin

Tasman Sea

PACIFIC OCEAN

New Zealand

New Zealand is a tiny
wine producing country;
however, the quality and
purity of its wines command
respect far and wide. It took until the 1970s for the coin
to drop that despite the problems of growing grapes in
New Zealand's cool climate, such conditions were ideal
for producing fresh, crisp, aromatic dry white wines.

Although vines were planted in New Zealand in the nineteenth century, the general assumption seems to have been that the climate was too cold for large-scale commercial wine production.

Varietals and wines

The variety that has flourished most in this cool maritime environment is of course the Sauvignon Blanc. Some impressive Chardonnays are also being made. More controversial are the red wines. The right sort of varieties have been planted including Cabernet Sauvignon, Merlot and Pinot Noir, but with a cool climate there are going to be years when late ripening varieties are going to struggle. That said, the corner may have been turned in 1998. The growing season was very warm that year, so the grapes were ripe at harvest and some fine reds have been produced.

Wine producing areas

The warmer North Island is the historic home of the New Zealand wine industry, with many large companies being based in the Auckland area. However, the North Island's main vineyards lie along the east coast. Gisborne was traditionally a bulk wine area where a lot of Müller-Thurgau was planted. South of Gisborne is Hawkes Bay, New Zealand's key red wine producing area. Just outside Wellington is the Martinborough region, the origin of New Zealand's finest Pinot Noirs.

At the north end of the South Island is Marlborough, which is now the largest wine region in New Zealand. This vineyard area is where most of the Sauvignon Blanc is planted. Bordered by mountains on both sides, the Wairau Valley has a cool, dry climate. As you venture south on the South Island the climate is getting cooler. Vineyards have been planted near Christchurch and as far south as Central Otago.

SOUTH AND EAST ASIA

Despite the risk of fungal diseases brought on by its humid climate, Japan does make some wines, but these are rarely if ever exported.

The production of wine from grapes is still a small business in China. Several of the newer wineries are the result of joint ventures with western companies and some decent Chardonnays have already been produced.

India has had some success producing sparkling wines.

Best Buy

Villa Maria Marlborough Sauvignon Blanc 2000

Pale greenish straw. An intense, verging on pungent, nose. Packed with green fruit: apples, pears and gooseberries. Other aromas include cut grass, pea pods and asparagus. Dry, mid-high acidity, highish alcohol. Fairly light-bodied. Similar strong 'green' flavours to those picked up on the nose. Moderate length.

A fantastic piece of domestic architecture tucked into one of the Hawkes Bay vineyards.

American vines	Species of vine originating in the eastern part of North America (e.g. *Vitis rupestris*). Can be used to make wine, but more often used as rootstocks for *Vitis vinifera*.
Ampelography	The study of the vine.
Aspersion	Spraying the vines with water to minimise damage from spring frost.
Assemblage	Blending.
Autovinifier	A fermentation vat that uses the carbon dioxide generated by the fermentation to pump itself over.
Barrique	A 225 litre (59 US gallon) oak barrel.
Basket press	A press with a vertical action.
Bâtonnage	Lees stirring whilst a wine is in barrel.
Baumé	A scale of sweetness used when measuring the sugar content of grape must.
Bentonite	Type of clay used to fine white wine.
Bio-dynamic viticulture	A radical version of organic viticulture, where the timing of vineyard and winery activities is determined by factors like the lunar cycle.
Biological control	The use of natural predators to control pests.
Blind tasting	Tasting wine without knowing the identity of what is in the glass.
Bloom	The waxy film on the skin of the grape, composed in part of wild yeast.
Bodega	A warehouse or winery.
Bordeaux mixture	The spray traditionally used to prevent Downy Mildew. It is composed of copper sulphate, lime and water.
Botrytis cinerea	The fungus that is responsible for both Grey Rot and Noble Rot.
Boutique winery	A small, newly established winery that sells over-priced wines.
Brix	A scale of sweetness used when measuring the sugar content of grape must.
Bush vine	A free-standing spur-pruned vine.

Butt	The large barrel, about 550 litres (145 US gallons) used for maturing Sherry.
Cane pruning	A pruning system in which the vine is pruned back to leave one or more canes, each of which possesses approximately six buds.
Cap	The layer of skins that forms at the surface of fermenting red wine.
Carbonic maceration	A technique used to produce red wines with less tannin than a conventional vinification. Whole bunches of black grapes are sealed in a vat in an atmosphere saturated with carbon dioxide.
Chai	A building for storing barrels.
Chaptalisation	The addition of sugar to the grape must just before or during fermentation. This sugar is converted into alcohol, raising the strength of the finished wine. N.B. This is not a method for producing sweet wine.
Charmat method	The tank method of sparkling wine production.
Château	A wine producing estate.
Chêne	Oak.
Chlorosis	A vine disease caused by a lack of iron in the soil.
Clone	A particular strain of a grape variety.
Cold treatment	The refrigeration of wine just before bottling to crystallise out any excess salts of tartaric acid.
Cordon training	This is where a spur-pruned vine has been trained on wires.
Corked	A wine that has cork taint.
Coulure	The abortion of grapes at flowering leading to a loss of crop.
Cross	A vine produced by crossing two varieties of *Vitis vinifera*.
Cru	A vineyard (sometimes translated into English as 'growth').
Cultured yeast	Strains of yeast that have been isolated, purified and cultured for use in the winery.

Cuvaison	Leaving a red wine with its skins after fermentation to extract more colour and tannin.
Cuve	Vat or tank.
Cuve close	The tank method of sparkling wine production.
Cuvée	Blend. In Champagne the word 'cuvée' is also the name given to the first pressing.
Cuverie / Cuvier	Vat house.
Débourbage	Settling of the grape must before fermentation.
Dégorgement	The removal of the sediment from a bottle of Champagne.
Domaine	A wine producing estate.
Dosage	The amount of sugar added to Champagne in the *liqueur d'expédition*. The sweetness of a Champagne is determined by the level of dosage.
Downy Mildew	A fungal disease that attacks all the green parts of the vine.
Eclaircissage	See 'Green harvesting'.
Edelfäule	Noble Rot (*see entry*).
En primeur	The sale of wine whilst it is still maturing in barrel or vat.
Estufagem	The heating stage in the production of Madeira.
European vine	*Vitis vinifera*, the species of vine responsible for most of the world's wine production.
Fining	The process used to clarify wine.
Free run wine	The red wine that drains out of a fermentation vat under gravity.
Fût	A barrel.
Garage wines	Newly created, violently expensive Bordeaux wines produced in tiny quantities.
Generics	Wines named primarily after their region of origin, cf. 'Varietals'.
Gobelet	A spur-pruned vine (sometimes trained up a post).

Grafting	The process of taking a cutting of a *Vitis vinfera* vine and grafting it on to a pest-resistant rootstock. *Phylloxera* and Nematodes are dealt with by grafting. If the grafting is done at the nursery the process is referred to as 'bench grafting'. When carried out in the vineyard it is called 'field grafting'.
Grape spirit	Water white, newly distilled, grape brandy.
Green harvesting	Summer crop thinning. By reducing the yield in this way the hope is that the remaining grapes will produce a more concentrated wine.
Grey Rot	A highly destructive fungal disease of the grape.
Guyot	A vine pruning and training system, in which a cane-pruned vine is trained along wires.
Gyropalette	The automated system of *remuage*.
Hybrid	A vine produced by crossing a *Vitis vinifera* vine with a vine of another species.
Hydrometer	An instrument used for measuring the density of a liquid. It is used in the winery to determine the sugar content of grape must, and the alcohol content of wine.
Injection method	The sparkling wine production method in which carbon dioxide is simply pumped into the base wine.
Lactic acid	The soft, buttery acidity found in wines that have undergone malolactic fermentation.
Lagar	The trough used in Portugal for treading the grapes.
Lees	The sediment in the bottom of a vat or barrel.
Liqueur d'expédition	A mixture of wine and sugar. This is the topping-up liquid added to Champagne just before the final cork is driven in.
Liqueur de tirage	A mixture of wine, sugar and yeast. This liquid is added to the base wine of Champagne to stimulate the second fermentation.
Lodge	A warehouse used for maturing Port or Madeira.
Macération carbonique	Carbonic maceration (*see entry*).

Malic acid	The sharp, appley acidity found in grapes, and in wines that have not undergone malolactic fermentation.
Malolactic fermentation or 'MLF'	The transformation of malic acid into lactic acid by bacteria.
Marc	The mass of dry skins and pips left after the pressing.
Méthode Champenoise	The old-fashioned name for the traditional method of sparkling wine production. *See 'Traditional method'*.
Méthode traditionelle	The traditional method of sparkling wine production *See 'Traditional method'*.
Microclimate	The climate experienced in a particular vineyard, rather than in a region as a whole.
Millerandage	The failure of pollination at flowering leading to a loss of crop.
Mousse	Sparkle.
Must	Grape juice.
Natural wine yeast	Strains of yeast found naturally in wineries that can ferment wines to completion.
Nematodes	Microscopic worms that attack the roots of the vine.
New World	The wine producing countries of the Americas, Australasia and Southern Africa.
Noble Rot	Fungal infection of the grape, which by concentrating the grape sugars allows the production of sweet wines like Sauternes.
Oechsle	A scale of sweetness used when measuring the sugar content of grape must.
Oenology	The science of wine.
Off trade	Supermarkets, off-licences and other operations that sell wine for consumption in the home.
Oidium	Powdery Mildew (*see entry*).
Old World	The wine producing countries of Europe, North Africa and the Middle East.
On trade	Establishments where you drink on their premises, e.g. restaurants, hotels, pubs and clubs.
Organic viticulture	Growing vines without the use of synthetic fertilisers or pesticides.
Out-of-condition or 'OOC'	A faulted wine.
Oxidation	The reaction of a wine with atmospheric oxygen. Heavy oxidation ruins most wines, although Oloroso Sherry gets much of its character from this process.
Passito	The drying of grapes (usually indoors) for the production of sweet wines.
Peronospera	Downy Mildew (*see entry*).
Pétillant	Slightly sparkling.
Phylloxera vastatrix	The vine louse. This pest is kept at bay by grafting *Vitis vinifera* vines on to American rootstocks.
Pigeage	Punching down the cap of skins at the surface of a fermenting red wine.
Pipe	The large barrel, about 550 litres (145 US gallons) used for maturing Port.
Pneumatic press	A modern type of press in which the grapes are gently squeezed by the inflation of a rubber bag.
Pourriture grise	Grey Rot (*see entry*).
Pourriture noble	Noble Rot (*see entry*).
Powdery Mildew	A fungal disease that attacks all the green parts of the vine.
Press wine	The darkly coloured and tannic red wine squeezed out of the skins after fermentation.
Pupitre	The wooden racks used for carrying out the *remuage* of Champagne by hand.
Quinta	A wine producing estate.
Racking	Draining a wine out of a vat or barrel.
Rectified concentrated must or 'RCM'	The concentrated and purified grape must used as a sweetening agent.
Refractometer	An instrument that uses the light refracting property of sugar to measure its concentration in grape must.

Remontage	Pumping over. During a red wine fermentation, wine is taken from the bottom of the vat, pumped up and then sprayed over the cap of skins.
Remuage	Driving the yeast sediment in a bottle of Champagne down to the cork.
Residual sugar	The sugar remaining in a wine after the end of fermentation. The more residual sugar, the sweeter the wine.
Rootstock	The bottom part of a graft. In vines the rootstock will usually be an American vine.
Scion	The top part of a graft. In vines the scion will be a cutting of *Vitis vinifera*.
Solera system	The extraordinary blending and maturation system used in the production of Sherry.
Spur pruning	A pruning system in which the vine is pruned back to leave two or more spurs, each of which possesses two or three buds.
Sulphur dioxide	The key preservative used in winemaking. It kills yeast and bacteria, and is an anti-oxidant.
Süssreserve	The unfermented grape must used to sweeten many German wines.
Taille	The second pressing in Champagne.
Tank method	The sparkling wine production method where the carbon dioxide is generated by a second fermentation in a sealed vat.
Tannin	The mouth-drying substance extracted from the skins of black grapes and therefore found in all red wines.
Tartaric acid	The principal acid found in both grapes and wine.
Tartrate crystals	The harmless, naturally occurring crystals sometimes found in bottled wine. They are composed of the salts of tartaric acid.
Terroir	The vine's immediate growing environment. The term encompasses soil, aspect and microclimate.

Traditional method	The sparkling wine production method in which the carbon dioxide is generated by a second fermentation in bottle. The yeast sediment is removed by *remuage* and *dégorgement*.
Transfer method	This sparkling wine production method is similar to the traditional method in that the carbon dioxide is generated by a second fermentation in bottle. However, in the transfer method the yeast is removed by emptying the bottles, filtering out the yeast and then re-bottling in a fresh bottle.
Triage	Sorting of grapes in the vineyard or at the winery to eliminate any sub-standard fruit.
Tris	Multiple waves of selective picking as employed in the production of Noble Rot wines.
Unit of alcohol	8 g (¼ oz) of alcohol. A 125 ml (4 fl oz) glass of wine at 12%ABV contains 1.5 units of alcohol.
Varietals	Wines named primarily after their grape variety(ies), cf. 'Generics'.
Véraison	The moment when ripening black grapes change colour.
Vinification	Wine making.
Viticulture	Grape growing.
Vitis vinifera	The European vine, which is used to produce most of the world's wine.
Volatile acidity or 'VA'	Acetic acid. All wines contain traces of acetic acid. However, if the smell of acetic acid is prominent on the nose of a wine then it is out of condition (acetic acid is the principal component of vinegar).
Vendange verte	See 'Green harvesting'.
Wild yeast	The naturally occurring yeast found on the grape skin.
Yeast autolysis	The breakdown of the yeast in the sediment of a bottle of Champagne during its maturation. This process is responsible for many of the complex aromas found on the nose of a fine Champagne.

Recommended reading & Useful contacts

Books

Beeston, John. *The Wine Regions of Australia*. Allen & Unwin, 1999.

Belfrage, Nicolas. *Barolo to Valpolicella: The Wines of Northern Italy*. Faber, 1999. (The second volume covering Southern Italy is to be published soon.)

Bird, David. *Understanding Wine Technology*. DBQA Publishing, 2000.

Biss, Austen & Smith, Owen. *The Wines of Chablis*. Writers International, 2000.

Blom, Philipp. *The Wines of Austria*. Faber, 2000.

Brook, Stephen. *The Wines of California*. Faber, 1999.

Cernilli, Daniele and Petrini, Carlo. *Italian Wines*. Gambero Rosso and Slow Food Editore, published annually.

Coates, Clive. *Côte d'Or: A Celebration of the Great Wines of Burgundy*. Weidenfeld & Nicolson, 1997.

Coates, Clive. *Grands Vins: The Finest Châteaux of Bordeaux and their Wines*. Weidenfeld & Nicolson, 1995.

Duijker, Hubrecht. *The Wine Atlas of Spain*. Mitchell Beazley, 1992.

Duijker, Hubrecht. *Wines of Chile*. Mitchell Beazley, 2000.

Halliday, James. *Australia & New Zealand Wine Companion*. Grub Street, published annually.

Hanson, Anthony. *Burgundy*. Faber, new edn 1995.

Irvine, Ronald with Clore, Walter. *The Wine Project: Washington State's Winemaking History*. Sketch Publications, 1997.

Jeffs, Julian. *Sherry*. Faber, 4th edn, 1992.

Johnson, Hugh. *The Atlas of German Wines*. Mitchell Beazley, 1986.

Johnson, Hugh. *Pocket Wine Book*. Mitchell Beazley, published annually.

Johnson, Hugh. *The Story of Wine*. Mitchell Beazley, 1989.

Johnson, Hugh and Robinson, Jancis. *The World Atlas of Wine*. Mitchell Beazley, 5th edn, 2001.

Lemay, Marc-Henry. *Bordeaux et Ses Vins*. Editions Féret, 15th edn, 1995.

Liddell, Alex. *Madeira*. Faber, 1998.

Mayson, Richard. *Port and the Douro*. Faber, 1999. (Richard is also writing a general book on Portuguese wine.)

Norman, Remington. *Rhône Renaissance*. Mitchell Beazley, 1995.

Pintarich, Paul. *The Boys Up North: Dick Erath and the early Oregon winemakers*. The Wyatt Group, 1997.

Radford, John. *The New Spain*. Mitchell Beazley, 1998.

Ribereau-Gayon, Pascal (ed.). *Hachette Wine Guide*. Hachette UK, published annually (published in France as *Le Guide Hachette des Vins*).

Robinson, Jancis. *Vines, Grapes and Wines*. Mitchell Beazley, 1986.

Robinson, Jancis (ed.). *The Oxford Companion to Wine*. Oxford, new edn, 1999.

Spence, Godfrey. *The Port Companion*. Apple, 1997.

Stevenson, Tom. *Alsace*. Faber, 1993.

Stevenson, Tom. *The New Sotheby's Wine Encyclopedia*. Dorling Kindersley, 1997.

Stevenson, Tom. *World Encyclopedia of Champagne & Sparkling Wine*. Christie's / Absolute Press, 1998.

Strang, Gavin. *Wines of South-West France*. Kyle Cathie, 1996.

Stuttaford, Thomas. *To Your Good Health! The Wise Drinker's Guide*. Faber, 1997.

Unwin, Tim. *Wine & The Vine: An Historical Geography of Viticulture and the Wine Trade*. Routledge, 1991.

van Zyl, Philip (ed.). *John Platter South African Wines*. Newsome McDowall, published annually.

Waldin, Monty. *Organic Wine Guide*. Thorsons, 1999.

Young, Alan. *The Wine Routes of Argentina*. International Wine Academy, 1998.

Magazines

Decanter and *Wine* are the UK's two main glossy consumer wine magazines. Both have in-depth articles on all aspects of wine, interspersed with the results of blind wine tastings. *Wine Spectator* is the corresponding US consumer publication. Robert Parker, the highly respected American wine guru, publishes his thoughts in *The Wine Advocate*. *The Vine* is the equivalent publication of British Master of Wine, Clive Coates. Subscription details can be found at the following websites: www.decanter.com, www.wine-magazine.co.uk, www.winespectator.com, www.wineadvocate.com and www.clive-coates.co.uk Information about *The Wine & Spirit Diary* is available at www.winediary.com

Useful contacts – wine education and information on the web

Wine education

A key contact if you want to learn more about wine is The Wine & Spirit Education Trust (WSET). Based in London, the WSET runs courses all around the UK. What is more, its courses are offered by colleges and individuals in many other countries as well. Details can be found at www.wset.co.uk

Websites

The following websites are well worth a browse:

www.winespectator.com – a great site run by the *Wine Spectator* magazine. Lots of news, wine assessments, general information, vintage reports etc.

www.decanter.com – linked to *Decanter* magazine, like the *Wine Spectator* site it contains a mass of useful information.

www.jancisrobinson.com – Jancis Robinson, MW has an encyclopaedic knowledge of wine. Her independent wine assessments and reviews are well worth consulting.

www.wine-pages.com – Tom Cannavan's site is a real mine of information. It's all there: book reviews, an Internet forum, links etc.

www.cyberbacchus.com – an extremely good jumping off point with thousands of links to winery websites. www.allaboutwine.com and www.winesite.co.uk are also very good for their links.

www.localwineevents.com – at a loose end? This site will have details of a wine-related gig near you.

www.bonnydoonvineyard.com – my favourite site.

Index

190

Index

For Ruth, Ellen and Elizabeth

Acknowledgements

picture credits

Michelle Garrett/HarperCollins*Publishers* pp. 2, 4, 6, 8, 11, 12, 16–17, 21, 25, 27, 28, 30, 64,68–9, 71, 91,127, 140–1; Frank Wieder/HarperCollins*Publishers* pp. 5 (top) 29

All location photography supplied by Cephas Picture Library. Photographs by Mick Rock except: Andy Christodolo pp. 36, 52, 108, 145, 168; Kevin Judd pp. 156, 161, 179; Herve Champollion p. 154; Juan Espi p. 172; Bruce Fleming p. 41; Walter Geierserger p. 147 and Alain Proust p. 171.

author's and publisher's acknowledgements

A special thank you to Denise Parker at Carlsberg-Tetley for their generous donation of most of the wine used during photography and Roger Burton at Riedel Crystal for the supply of glasses. Thank you also to all the following people: Charles Taylor, MW; Nick Belfrage, MW, at Vinexus Limited; Mike Hothersall at Codorniu (UK) Limited; Lee Gould at Matthew Clark; Philip Tuck, MW at Hatch Mansfield Agencies; Robin Walters, MW at John E Fells & Sons Limited; Su-Lin Ong on behalf of Maxxium UK Limited; and David Gleave, MW at Liberty Wines (UK) Limited.

Project Editor	Silvija Davidson
Layout Editors	Kathy Steer and Jo Lethaby
Project Designer	Kathy Gammon
Layout Designer	Liz Brown
Cartographer	Olive Pearson
Photographer	Michelle Garrett
Photographer's Assistant	Dulcie Ribero